To Ben,

Molly x

Facebook Me myself and ADHD
Instagram mollyadhdmayhem
YouTube Mollys Adhd Mayhem


**This book is dedicated to my beautiful Nan
and my fur bestie westie who sadly passed away:
DEXTER.**

# CONTENTS PAGE...

# INTRODUCTION

Firstly, let me introduce myself, I'm Paula (Molly's mum) I'm writing a little introduction on behalf of myself and my husband Ray (Molly's dad).

Molly was a very wanted baby. Myself and her dad struggled to conceive and just as we were going to be giving up fertility treatment, we were gifted a beautiful strawberry blonde baby girl. Molly was born on the 11th of June 1998. BUT little did we know the challenges we were going to be facing along Molly's journey through life.

Molly never believed in herself. Not everyone believed in Molly, BUT we did. We knew just how amazingly talented and passionate she was. She has gone on to really make us proud and she has achieved astounding things despite all her personal challenges!

Molly has inspired a lot of people by not letting anything stop her from achieving her dreams and by being a kind, and caring person. We hope you enjoy Molly's journey with ADHD, and I hope that you can see how amazing Molly is just like all her family do!

We wouldn't change Molly for the world!

Happy reading

Paula and Ray

# MOLLY

My name is Molly, I am 22 years old. I have ADHD.

*This is me ...*
*Well, it was a few years ago - back when I was at school. I have chosen to write this book about ME and my personal experiences. I have chosen my book to be focused on my school life, and behaviour and trust me it gets REALLY INTERESTING.*
*I hope you enjoy it! Please let me know by following my Facebook blog page and YouTube channel and telling me you enjoyed it - Me myself and ADHD.*

This book is going to be about my crazy life experiences with **ADHD**. It's going to be an honest and raw insight into my school life, along with some really embarrassing, rebellious school topics that you usually wouldn't tell your parents. (sorry **MUM** and **DAD** if you're reading this).

My goal for this book is to help **YOU**. You are reading this book for a reason, so whether you're a parent, carer or even a teacher, I hope to create a more diverse understanding of how ADHD can feel, and how **MUCH** it can affect our daily lives.

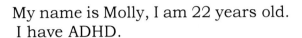

I'm going to be writing about some of the things that have caused me a lot of personal heartbreak and emotional exhaustion. Some of the topics include my friendships, behaviour problems and meltdowns and much more. So, I hope this book helps to raise the awareness that ADHD needs.

I have my own blog and I have had a lot of positive feedback about my posts, and have been told that they have helped parents, carers and even teachers, understand their children or students with ADHD better. This is what has inspired me to write my own book. I'm hoping that by communicating and sharing my personal experiences I can show others they aren't alone, and just how tough living with ADHD really is. I'm no professional, but I'm living with it and always will be living with it. I want to give you a look into my life, hoping that it will help you to understand your loved ones or students with ADHD. We aren't bad people; we are just incredibly misunderstood, and I want to try and change that.

By writing this I hope that my knowledge and personal experiences with my ADHD can give you the knowledge to give your own little ADHDers the support and guidance they need, so they do not feel so isolated and alone. My parents had to go through this completely alone, and they suffered a **LOT** with my behaviour problems and anxiety. I particularly want to give parents and carers some support, so they don't have to go through this alone like my parents did.

My aim is to give an honest and true representation and a realistic insight into our ADHD mindset: AKA my life. But most importantly I want to give my readers some of my very own tips, which I believe helped

me. In **NO** way am I saying it fixed my ADHD or cured it, but it certainly made my life easier. By sharing my own experiences, I hope to educate parents, carers, and teachers of children with ADHD. By doing that I hope they can learn new ways to understand their loved ones or students with ADHD and make their own lives easier. I also write about how ADHD can be just as beneficial as it is difficult.

I'm going to be writing about my symptoms and how they affected me in my infant years, and most importantly my school life. I want to write about my School life in depth as it was very difficult, not only for me but for **EVERYONE** involved. I want to be open and honest with you guys, as I know that I'm not the only one who has gone through this and I certainly won't be the last to go through what I did at school. I feel like school is a common thing most of us with ADHD struggle with **OR** have struggled with. School/college or in fact any educational setting, and the teachers in general is **NOT** an easy environment for those of us that suffer from ADHD to deal with. Authority and rules aren't easy for us to understand and obey, plus it's busy and **LOUD**. But others don't understand how **HARD** it actually is to live with ADHD and the complexities that come with it.

I have chosen **MY** personal experiences with school to be the main subject of my book because my issues were very difficult and dominated this time in my life. I feel that parents and teachers will benefit from reading my points of view and experiences. I was confused and scared. I was always known as the **NAUGHTY KID** and I was always getting myself into all kinds of trouble. Things only got worse as I got older. I was just a misunderstood child. My school life was where the majority of my behavioural problems were at their worst and most troublesome; my life just spiralled out of control and I want to help prevent others feeling like I did.

So, please enjoy and remember that YOU aren't alone, you have me. I'm here to spread some cheer on ADHD. **YOU CAN SIT BACK AND READ ALL MY FUNNY EXPERIENCES** and laugh at the fact that no one is NORMAL, and we just have to embrace our differences.

I hope this book brings you some knowledge, guidance, and helps you understand ADHD ... **ENJOY READING**.

*MOLLY X*

# ME, MYSELF, AND ADHD

Written by Molly Brooks-Dridge

# WHAT IS ADHD TO ME?

ADHD Is a tricky one to explain. All I can say, is if you have ever experienced a radio and a television on in the same room, at the same time and **BOTH** with the volume on full blast. That is pretty much an accurate representation of how my mind feels every day. It becomes very overwhelming, loud, and isolating at times. But throughout my life I have never had the support I needed to be able to "Tune" into the right radio station or pick the right television channel in my mind that would allow me to be the best version of myself. Unfortunately, my ADHD wasn't diagnosed until I was a young adult, which didn't help either.

ADHD isn't just about being the "naughty kid" or the "troublemaker" in the classroom. It is so much more than that, it's actually a very complex mental disorder ... and it's hard to get a correct diagnosis for it.

Girls are more likely to be misdiagnosed with teenage-Hormones or anxiety or even just self-esteem /confidence issues. Most girls do NOT get diagnosed until they are adults, which can make life a MASSIVE struggle to cope with alone, without any of the medication or support needed to help reduce the symptoms of ADHD.

But let's get on with what you guys came here to read, how it affects me.

## SO, WHERE DO I START?

Ever since I can remember I have had such an issue with making friends, even if I manage to make a friend, keeping them as my friend is an even bigger challenge for me personally. I would give my all to make someone happy and I'll do anything I can to make them like me. Sometimes this isn't my best quality as some people see it as obsessive and desperate.

I get **WAY** too attached to friends, this can also be seen as jealousy, as I can easily get upset when they have other friends, just because I know how easily I could be replaced.

I want to be doing something all the time. This can come across as annoying, as not everyone has the unlimited amount of energy I have. There are many things that put people off being my friend. Mostly, my impulsiveness which can become very overpowering.

I have always had a **HUGE** attachment issue to my Mum. I hated going anywhere alone, even being left at the school gates; even my mum just going out with friends or family without me. I guess I would say it's a type of separation anxiety. To this day it is still a **HUGE** issue for me.

I'm a 21-year-old (at the time of writing) who doesn't like being away from her Mum. I don't feel safe unless I'm with her; she is my best friend and my safety net, and I wouldn't change it for the world. I used to get  embarrassed that I don't like being away from her, even if it's just her going shopping. I become emotional and am sad that I'm not with her. I always have this awful feeling as though something bad is going to happen to me if she isn't by my side. Obviously, this has made having a job or any sort of an independent life extremely hard for me. I **HATE** it and I just can't cope without her for a long period of time.

I have always had a bad temper and I am always the first one to shout and scream if I'm not happy with a situation. However, what others don't understand, or even try to understand is that shouting, and screaming is also our coping mechanism. I can't always cope when all of my emotions start trying to dominate me. It's hard to control, so having a temper/argument is the only way it can come out. Sometimes, it's my (not just me, it's very common in ADHD) way of communicating when things get too **MUCH**. I have taught myself to hold my ADHD symptoms in A LOT; I have to hide them away from people who don't know me well enough as I don't feel comfortable telling people I suffer from ADHD. This can typically cause my anxiety or ADHD to "kick off" especially when Im at home. I can release all my feelings and they come out like a tsunami, there's no stopping me. Sometimes if you get caught by my tsunami of moods you could honestly drown from my anger and tears.

I was **NOT** exactly the brightest spark in school, but I didn't help myself either. I was Loud, had a bad attitude problem, but mostly I was misunderstood, I went through the whole of my education undiagnosed and DIFFERENT. Deep down I knew there was something wrong, so did my parents and my close mentors. I wanted a career in the police when I was older so me, and my parents decided alongside both my deputy head teachers at my secondary school, that we would try to improve my behaviour. We tried strategies like mentoring, report cards and rewards but that didn't help one bit. If I'm being honest, I think I enjoyed the extra attention I was receiving from all the teachers. I began to feel like I was untouchable.

**MY BEHAVIOUR WENT DOWN HILL SO FAST FROM HERE. LET ME TELL YOU SOME OF THE THINGS THAT I STARTED DOING & THAT BEGAN TO HAPPEN MORE AND MORE REGULARLY.**

• I started walking out of classes – simply getting up and walking out whenever I felt like it. I didn't care at all that I was ruining my education.

• Bunking classes - again like the one above, I didn't care that I was impacting my education, I felt like I was above the school rules. It gave me a buzz: a rush of adrenaline.

• Swearing at teachers and in class. If I felt like it, I would do it and to hell with the consequences!

• I was disruptive, and I was disrupting others who wanted to learn - I would talk, talk over people, laugh loudly, and shout. Run around and get others involved with my antics.

• I was running riot around school – I was never in my lesson, but I was always in places I shouldn't be.

• I was bringing banned items from home into school because I knew they weren't allowed; I got some type of kick out of it all.

• Eventually the school couldn't handle it and decided to exclude me for a period of time, and this was meant to help me, but it didn't. I had become unruly and it was starting to affect my family life massively and my family started to distance themselves from me. I was banned from school trips, P.E lessons etc. I was put on a part time timetable, which led on to me attending a pupil referral unit part time.

My dream career was becoming less and less likely to happen. I couldn't even follow simple instructions like "sit quietly in assembly," let alone being in the police force. I had Two teachers that had my back throughout my secondary school life. One of those teachers is named Mrs M (for identity purposes. I treated them both like absolute rubbish because I thought I was untouchable, and I just didn't care who or what was affected by my extremely rebellious behaviour. Mrs M was incredibly supportive and understanding, I'm going to tell you honestly that Mrs M has had an ongoing effect on my life. I wouldn't be who I am today without some of her wise words along with my Mum's support.

Anxiety will always be my biggest fight; it's something I have to battle every day. Eventually, I had to give up fighting and get help after I had a bad mental breakdown at the end of 2017 and 2018. I wasn't the type of person who believed in relying on Medication, but I have to now. I take antidepressants to help my day be that little bit easier for me to handle. I honestly couldn't cope anymore.

I can pinpoint the exact time my anxiety started. I let it win and I haven't had a fighting chance since. I was 12 years old and it has continued to slowly but surely ruin my life.

**I REALLY WANT THIS BOOK TO HELP PARENTS AND TEACHERS UNDERSTAND KIDS WITH ADHD IN MORE DEPTH. WE NEED YOU ARE ON OUR SIDE. WE CAN'T FIGHT THIS ON OUR OWN. I'M USING THIS BOOK TO BE "THEIR" VOICES, AS SOME KIDS CAN'T COMMUNICATE WHAT THEY ARE REALLY FEELING. SO, BY READING THIS HOPEFULLY I AM GIVING YOU AN IDEA OF WHAT IT'S LIKE IN THE MIND OF US, ADHD SUFFERERS.**

I will be going through all these subjects, such as, secondary school and all the trouble I caused in a lot more detail throughout my book. But this is just to explain what ADHD is and how it affected and affects me. I wanted to start from the very beginning so you can get to know how all my ADHD traits showed themselves from a very young age, and now I am going to get started with my **ADHD JOURNEY** ... But before we jump into that, I am going to be writing some of my personal experiences with life in general, written in a diary/blog style so it will be easier to navigate around the book ... so let's get going ...

# ME AND MY TRAITS

Being diagnosed with ADHD made complete sense to me. It came as **NO** surprise whatsoever to me that I officially had ADHD. Both, myself, and my parents had always suspected that I had some extra **FUNKY** ingredients added into my brain. I was silently suffering with what I now know to be my ADHD. But so were my parents, they certainly didn't sign up for what they got from me growing up; they didn't know what they had got themselves into but being diagnosed completely changed my life ... BUT for the right reasons. I have finally got the answers for some of the questions I used to ask myself.

- **WHAT** are the reasons for my quirkiness?
- **WHY** can't I make friends?
- **MOST** importantly why I'm different from my peers ... **VERY DIFFERENT**?

**(PLEASE REMEMBER I'M NOT A DOCTOR. Not everyone's ADHD traits are exactly the same. Always seek medical advice when diagnosing challenging behaviours.)**

**I WANT TO SHARE MY PERSONAL TRAITS.**

Why - you may ask?

 Because there will be some young children, teenagers, and young adults somewhere out there struggling from the same things, that I did at their age or possibly that I even still

do. ADHD doesn't just **STOP OVERNIGHT**. Someone could be silently struggling like I did or being **MISUNDERSTOOD** like I am. Sometimes just knowing you aren't alone **HELPS A LOT**. You might be able to get some comfort out of knowing that there are others suffering from **ADHD JUST LIKE YOU** - or your child!

**ASKING FOR HELP** can **REALLY HELP** too. Asking for help isn't a sign of weakness, actually it shows just how **STRONG** you are. Talking about your problems can seem really overwhelming. It can seem really hard at first, but **HONESTLY** the thing is, that once you start to admit that there is a problem you are on the right path to **SUCCESS**. It can be **SUPER** embarrassing opening-up and talking to someone. They might not FULLY understand how you really feel but **HONESTLY,** talking to someone can **HELP**. You will be able to get the support and guidance you need to carry on **SMASHING IT** in **LIFE**. ADHD doesn't have to define you. It's just a label. You can either let it take over your life, or you can benefit from the amazing things it offers.

**Some of the AMAZING Things ADHD offers can make you utterly desirable, for example -**

• Resilience and determination - Having ADHD makes things a bit trickier. So, we have to learn to be resilient to failure or rejection. When we get knocked down, we **have to** get straight back up again. We have the willpower to carry on and keep on trying to achieve our goals. We are determined to achieve anything we set our minds to.

• Creativity - Someone with ADHD can give you some amazing creative ideas that others might not think of. We can do this due to our ability to **HYPER FOCUS**. Someone with ADHD can bring amazing things to both group and individual projects such as: Energy ... new ways to approach projects and can be a useful person to bring with new ideas, methods, and strategies. We are a great asset to have in a group.

• Expression - We have the ability to express our emotions. Sometimes intensely, but we do really feel our emotions strongly. Whenever we are passionate about something, we give our **ALL** to achieve our goals. We are loving and caring. We are passionate about our family, friends and most importantly our pets. We are able to communicate how we feel, not only verbally but we can use our creativity to write poems and draw pictures; we have our own individual ways of expressing ourselves.

• Adaptable - We can fit in to a variety of different groups. We are able to do this because we mask our own differences. We try to fit in with our peers. We adapt our personalities to match those in the environment around me. We are like a human chameleon. We change to adapt to our current environment; to not be vulnerable, and to simply blend into society.

These are just a few of our incredible traits we have been gifted by our ADHD ... **WE ARE LUCKY**.

ADHD is **OUR** hidden **SUPERPOWER** trust me. Sometimes being impulsive and spontaneous is exactly what is needed.

## SO, HERE ARE THE MAJORITY OF MY TRAITS AND SYMPTOMS

Throughout this book I will be sharing more of my experiences with my symptoms in more depth and in different environments, such as at school, my home life and at college. But for now, here's a list of my traits and symptoms ...

• I find it really **HARD** to make friends.

• I can't commit to anything: hobbies, clubs and even some types of relationships. I get bored easily.

• I'm very impulsive and very demanding.

• I don't have very good concentration. I can be talking to someone and paying attention, but my mind is thinking about loads of other things at the same time ... Im replaying conversations in my mind that had happened weeks ago.

• I'm awful at eye contact, it makes me extremely uncomfortable. I find myself zoning out of the conversation, because I'm focusing so hard on the fact that I need to be looking at them in the eyes. It is overwhelmingly uncomfortable for me to keep direct eye contact with someone.

• I can't complete tasks efficiently. I can start focusing on the project and get really into it. I will also be really motivated to compete the task and accomplish the goals I set for myself in a decent time but then it all fizzes out. I end up losing all the motivation and determination I had at the beginning of the project. I seem to just give up, lose all interest. I get easily bored and distracted.

• Time management is **NOT** my thing, I physically cannot seem to get myself organised and out of the door on time. I don't prioritise things appropriately. I forget to do things and end up getting all frustrated and angry at myself, then I take it out on those around me.

• My mood changes so fast, it changes faster than you can say ADHD. I say horrible things and I can be quite volatile. I say things like 'I hope you die,' calling my sister and parents nasty names.

• I become very aggressive and angry. When I get angry, I punch walls and slam doors. Once, I slammed a door so hard I pulled it off the door frame. I punch myself hard out of pure anger.

• My anxiety is extremely bad. I have had therapy, but unfortunately it didn't work. I hated the group sessions. I was too focused on what others were saying about germs and their anxiety worries. It made me paranoid about new things that I hadn't worried about before the sessions.

• I'm forgetful. But on the other hand, I am extremely good at remembering things photographically, and by sequences. Also, music, rhyme and beat ...

• I physically can't sit still to watch a film or read a book ... (ironically, I can write them.)

- I have always had trouble sleeping. I have to sleep in my mum's room or bed. I have panic attacks if I'm not near her.

- I have attachment issues.

- I am emotionally sensitive.

- I hate crowded areas. It makes me feel like I'm sinking into the floor. I get paranoid that others are staring and judging me.

- I don't like silence; I like to have music playing when I'm sleeping and when I'm trying to concentrate.

- I have had trouble getting myself into a proper hygiene routine.

- I am emotionally sensitive but on the other hand I can't read other people's emotions. If I know that person, I get paranoid that I have done something to upset them.

- Continuous noises irritate me. For example: high pitch noises that last for a while. Likewise, loud bangs that are unexpected.

- I look for negative attention more than I do positive. I almost crave it; it's like an addiction to me. The more negative attention I got at school the better. For some reason it made my anxiety better. I feel like, if I try to do stuff like study or work hard, I am scared that I will end up disappointing others ... so I don't try.

- My sense of danger is limited. When I drive, I get over stimulated and become fearless. It's like I want an adrenaline rush, so I typically end up driving faster and more dangerously.

• I don't have any friends at ALL. I can become extremely attached. I then become jealous and it comes across as overly clingy and obsessive.

• My emotions are all over the place. I'm basically emotional unstable.

• I know when things are wrong but for some reason I do it anyway without caring about the consequences.

• I don't like eating out at restaurants because I get really worried that something bad is going to happen to me, like my food being poisoned or having an allergic reaction. I get so paranoid. It can almost get over-powering for me.

• I daydream **A LOT.**

• I Get frustrated very quickly.

• I lose motivation and determination quickly.

• I lose things **OFTEN**.

• I have a HOT TEMPER!!!

• I learn better when I am shown what to do, as I find it hard to process things. I like things to be explained clearly and sometimes more than once.

• If I am with a group of people, I always end up being the loudest person, the most dominant and overpowering person. I almost instantly become the clown. I feel like being the silly one makes me less likely, to be seen, as my true self. I have to try and fit in any way I can. Usually, its by being the class clown.

- I take all my frustrations out on people I love the most.

- I'm extremely messy.

- I always convince myself that I have something medically wrong with me. I convince myself that I have the worst illnesses known to man.

- I always try to please others. I have ended up buying other people things just to try and make them like me.

- I have self-esteem issues/confidence.

- I always compare myself others.

- I hate change, especially if I was excited about something.

- I can't stick at a job. I hate working. It's so hard for me because the pressure to follow rules and be the perfect employee creates even more anxiety. I have difficulties maintaining positive relationships with other colleagues and find myself feeling rejected and isolated from others; I am just different to others.

- I can't take criticism; I take it to heart.

- I can't relax. I find it hard to sit still. I can't switch off; my mind goes into over-drive and as a result my anxiety goes off the scale.

- Panic attacks are a huge part of my daily routine.

- I can't let go of the past.

- I don't like routines.

- I always want something more than what I've got, nothing is ever good enough.

- I never stop talking.

- I'm extremely Impulsive. If I get an idea, I have to do it **NOW**. It's like I have to do it otherwise my anger rises. I get aggravated.

- I take things too far. I never know when to stop.

- I struggle with getting started on a project (this book has taken ages!)

- I procrastinate.

- I distract others and myself.

- I'm hyperactive.

  - I'm hyper focused; I focus on things too much.

  - I struggle with maintaining energy levels.

- I'm socially awkward.

- I have a hot temper and a feisty attitude ... and I'm stubborn.

- I hate going out without my mum, for fear that something bad is going to happen to me.

- I can't handle relationships.

- I can't handle rejection.

- I have oppositional behaviour.

- I rub the palms of my hands together, to try to control my anxiety.

- When I get stressed or scared, I cover my eyes and my ears.

- Interrupt others, and I talk over people.

- I don't like talking on the phone.

- I'm impatient.

- I have poor money management skills.

- I always think about death, as the worst-case scenario.

- I finish people's sentences. Which annoys others.

- I struggle with getting to sleep.

- I have so many nightmares. My mind just can't relax.

**THESE ARE MY PERSONAL EXPERIENCES WITH ADHD. NOT EVERYTHING I SUFFER WITH IS GOING TO HAPPEN TO EVERYONE WITH ADHD. EVERY INDIVIDUAL HAS THEIR OWN PERSONAL EXPERIENCES.**

I am also being tested for autism so some of these traits may be related to autism but right now I only have the official diagnosis of ADHD, so I blame ADHD ... **HAHA!**

**THAT SAID, I'M PROUD OF MY ADHD.**
However, my ADHD can be extremely hard for me to handle from day to day.

I have days when I might be feeling so angry and irritated and other days when I could be feeling emotionally vulnerable. My emotions can be very uncontrollable.

I can have days that I'm feeling under pressure and down about my life.

I have days where I continuously compare myself to other people that are "doing better" than I believe I am. I am going to give you a mixture of things that I personally find hard about my ADHD. I have written more in depth about some of my hardest challenges with **MY ADHD**.

I'm going to write a little about the most intense and challenging ones ... and what I find helps me deal with the impulsiveness, obsessiveness and all my traits in general.

**I'll start by listing most of my traits I have:**

•       **Impulsiveness** - this has to be, one of the hardest traits I struggle with. I can't just want something … it has to be like … I have to have it **NOW**. There's no reasoning with my mind. It's hard for me as I can't help being so impulsive, but even though I can't help it, I don't want to be like it. I would love to be able to save for something and get that sense of achievement but instead it always ends in tears or arguments. If someone says they don't think it's a good idea I get really angry because I have this rage inside me that just craves it. It's like not giving someone their drug fix; it's that strong of a feeling. When I am being impulsive, I don't think about the consequences, like what will happen later on when the next month's bills need to be paid. I just think about the here and now, the only thing I can think about is how much **I NEED** that particular thing.

•       **Low frustration and mood swings** - I can go from being really happy to be being really angry in seconds. It's scary how fast things can change. I can be triggered by the smallest of things, like the noise of someone eating, someone talking over me, simply feeling like someone isn't listening to me, things not going my way, being hungry. Literally, I have such irrational mood swings. If I've had something on my mind and I get excited or become really obsessed with something and someone tries to tell me I can't have it or do it, I get very angry because I want things to just happen my way or not at all; and every time I take it out on the people who love me the most.

•       **Obsession** - This is also a huge thing for me. This is something I believe could potentially be an autistic trait of mine as well. I have an obsession with cars. Not the make and models of cars as such but for some reason the feeling probably because when I passed my test I had loads of "friends." So, I always want another car because I believe it will make people like me and I will have my independence back.

- **Having no fear** - This is currently why I don't have a car. I was a **HUGE** danger on the road. I didn't care that I was driving over the speed limit. I had absolutely no fear. I would challenge myself in any way possible when I was driving. I wasn't scared of the police, I didn't care about my safety or my passengers, or even the other road user's safety. I was a cocky and dangerous driver. I would be out driving late at night. I didn't care that I had restrictions on my insurance and a black box. Which ended up with huge amounts of money being added on to my monthly direct debt because I would go over the allowed mileage that was set by the insurance company. I was fined for speeding and dangerous driving. In the end as a family we decided that selling the car was the best option, otherwise I doubt I would still be alive today if I were to have carried on driving the way I was.

- **I talk over people ALL time** - It comes across as obnoxious, but I just think I'm helping them finish the sentence. I know it's rude and it's an awful trait to have because I know how annoying and patronising it is, as I personally HATE people doing it to me.

 - **EYE contact** - has always been a huge issue for me. When I was at school all the teachers used to pick up on it and say you don't even listen to me when I'm talking to you, you are looking around the room and its SOOO rude.

It has got better since I started working with the public. It comes more naturally when I'm in a uniform and when they are asking me about train times as they are hoping I can help them which makes it a little easier. And because I don't know them it also seems help as well.

- **Jealousy/pure anger**. - I found that having a sibling means I compare myself to her, like when she goes out with her friends or has a boyfriend. I become very jealous and angry because I want that. When she started driving lessons, I became so selfish because all I could think about was myself. I can sometimes take the shine off of her achievements, as I get so angry and jealous that she doesn't want to talk about things around me, because she is scared, I'll shout at her. It hurts, because I just want to be happy for her, but I can't. I am getting so angry just thinking about it now. I get a knot in my stomach because I feel like she is achieving more than me, and that she has something I don't have. This happens with people I know if they get a car or have something, I think I need or want. I become so jealous it makes me so angry and changes my whole mood for the day because I feel like I am failing because of that one thing I don't have. I hate this as I seem so selfish, but I just can't help it.

- **Self-esteem** - Is an issue to the point that I have an acute eating disorder. I don't like to eat as I think being skinny is what makes you have friends ... and boyfriends. It is something that has recently started so it's still very raw to me, but I really believe that beauty is about your body size and weight. I don't want to talk about this massively as it's something that is seriously affecting my mental health. My parents are also affected by this and I don't want to upset anyone who is close to me reading this.

- **I have no organisation** - I get up about 15 mins before actually needing to leave for work and wonder why I'm always so rushed and forget things in the mornings. I get the same train every day to work, I know exactly when it leaves, I'm aware it usually leaves earlier but I still have no sense of urgency.
- I have problems with separation anxiety.

- Sleeping is a problem for me.

- I over think things.

- I suffer with mood swings.

- Poor time management.

- Laziness/Hygiene is always an issue.

- Depression and anxiety.

- I am hot headed.

- **Nothing comes naturally to me** - I can't read a book. I can't sit down and colour or any activities that require a lot of mental concentration ... (writing this I have been changing the songs, looking on Facebook).

- **Friendships and relationships** - Are another major issue for me. I could plan my life with someone without even knowing what their intentions are. They could have just liked my photo on social media, and I will automatically think they are either my friend or want me to be their girlfriend. There is **NO** in between. It's dangerous sometimes.

There's many more but these are the ones that I feel have the most impact on my daily life.

**So here are some things I find helpful for me:**

•        **Headphones** are never far away from me. I have earphones in all the time, it gives me some type of comfort.

•        I put a **hoodie** on and put the hood up and just lay down and watch YouTube.

•        **YouTube** is my favourite coping mechanism to do when I'm anxious or angry. Whatever the cause is, watching YouTube really helps me get myself under control and calm down. I usually watch vlogs and documentaries.

•        **Netflix** is another one of my coping mechanisms. I watch a series called The Gilmore girls, I have watched the whole series about 15/20 times, it somehow keeps my anxiety under control. I can connect to the characters and just really enjoy it; I watch many series on Netflix over, and over again. It is really unlikely, that I will just sit down and watch the tv or iPad, I usually just have it on as background noise because it is something, I find extremely relaxing.

•        **Math** revision is weirdly another thing I have recently come to find out keeps me focused, hours can go by and I'm so invested in doing well, that I no longer remember what I was worrying or angry about. I find it

relaxing, well, only if I've taken my medication, otherwise I wouldn't even be able to revise for 5 minutes without getting bored.

• **Graphic design** is a great way to keep myself occupied for a good few hours.

• **Going out with my mum**, is my most favourite type of therapy. My mum understands me so much. I can just be who I am, and she doesn't judge me or make me feel like I'm overreacting.

• **Taking my dog woody out** for a walk or even just cuddling him.

• **Music** sometimes helps but it isn't something that I would necessarily say helps me a lot.

**Obviously, I previously mentioned I am now medicated for my ADHD ... I am on a tablet called ELVANSE.**

It is an amphetamine-based stimulant. I'm obviously not promoting medication. I have personally chosen to take medication because at this moment in time it is in my best interests to do so.

**Medication has helped me. My family life is so much better.**

I can finally go out with my family and they are all enjoying my company, instead of walking on eggshells waiting for my next melt down. Which is usually the reason we end up going home early or not going out at all. My diagnosis has been a long time coming. Now I finally have it, I have become a lot more aware of all my traits. I have so many questions, but I don't have the answers to everything. So, me writing this is helping me get to grips with my own illness.

If you know someone that has ADHD, or actually any mental health issues, remember to always accept them and allow them to be themselves. When we are ourselves, around you, we feel very vulnerable. We don't just let our guards down to anybody. You should feel very honoured. We obviously trust you deeply. We only allow ourselves to be vulnerable around people we love and trust.

## ME AND MY ADHD AND EMOTIONS AREN'T A GOOD MIX.

Feelings are hard enough to Deal with when you don't have ADHD, but when you mix ADHD in with everyday emotions it can really make life a real struggle. Those of us with **ADHD FEEL** Rejection **A LOT**.

Rejection and intense emotional thoughts can be really difficult, when you have to live with ADHD 24/7. The hardest thing is that nobody understands us. It can be a real dark and lonely place on our worse days.

I find understanding and reacting appropriately to other's emotions very tricky. I either show way too much affection or I turn it around on me and start talking about my issues. My awareness of emotions is intense but appropriately approaching others to offer/receive help and comfort is a massive task.

Facial expressions and understanding other's intentions towards me are a complete mystery. Also, other people's tones of voice are puzzling, I can take things too much to heart. I suppose you could say I'm sensitive. When I misunderstand people's tones of voice it can cause arguments, simply because my misunderstanding is mistaken for obnoxiousness. The truth is that I just can't understand whether I've personally done something to you, or you're genuinely just not happy with everyone.

Socially this is my biggest struggle. I always get involved with the wrong people who bring out te worst in my ADHD. They encourage my bad symptoms and once they are released it's hard trying to round them all back up. Sometimes, I feel like I'm going to explode with emotions. It's like I can get a rush of all the emotions at once. It gets very over whelming and it becomes very hard to control mentally. Sometimes, having a meltdown is the only way of us expressing those suppressed emotions.

It's hard to explain our emotions at times, as it's not always easy to communicate how we are feeling. Sometimes there just isn't a name for the emotions we are feeling. Often, it's like an emotional journey all within one day. It can be really intense and messy inside our minds, especially if you can't verbally explain how you feel. So, imagine how easy it is for young children to be misunderstood by teachers, peers, and parents. Sometimes it is easier to just hurt those around you than it is to try and explain what's going on inside our minds. At times people with mental health issues have such strong stubborn minds which are hard for them to control. Once the emotions start freaking out that's when the meltdowns, physical, and verbal abuse start to happen, it's our way of controlling those intense emotional outbursts.

Anyway ... 80% of people that are Diagnosed with ADHD also have 1 or more of the following behavioural conditions. As if it isn't already enough of a complex disorder, there are so many other conditions that co-Exist with ADHD.

For example:

- Autism.
- OCD - obsessive compulsive disorder.
- Depression.

- Anxiety.
- Bipolar disorder.
- ODD -oppositional defiant disorder.
- Rejection sensitivity dysphoria.
- Tourette's syndrome.
- Disruptive mood disorder.

**And many more ...**

So, I had a phone call with my ADHD specialist, and I was telling her about my concerns and worries. I told her that I am 100% happy with my medication. I didn't plan on saying anything about ... what I'm about to tell you, but none the less I did. It came out naturally, so went with it and I was happy that it did come out. I usually wouldn't say anything, but as a result we decided to refer me to An Autism assessment.

I have been feeling like there's something else "different" about me recently, I just haven't felt "Myself." I'm still on my long-term dosage of medication and we have played around with my Anxiety medication but for some reason I just don't feel like I'm 100% "Fixed." (I know I'll never be fixed as I'm not broken but it's the only way, I can explain it.)

**Anyway, when I was speaking to the ADHD specialist, I mentioned that:**

- I feel so different to everyone else.
- I am so jealous of my younger sister.
- I just don't **understand** why I am not like others my age.
- I struggle with my work situation.
- Socially I struggle.
- I can't be myself around others.

I told her that I still don't feel 100% sure that we have all the right things diagnosed, I have researched **A LOT!** I emotionally and reluctantly opened-up to her and told her that I felt like there is something a **LOT** more than just ADHD going on with me. So, I'm now waiting for an Autism assessment. My ADHD assessment wasn't on the NHS, as I was on a waiting list for 2.5 years so, with my parents help I saved up and paid for a private diagnosis. I have been told that it will more than likely be a **WHILE**. for the autism assessment. But thankfully now I have the support of my parents to get me through the hard times. Although, even after speaking to my doctor, I'm still not fully convinced that I just have ADHD and (**MAYBE**) autism. I also believe there is a possibility I have PDA (Pathological Demand Avoidance) and ODD (Oppositional Defiance Disorder).

I really struggle with **A LOT** of things; but the things that get me stressed and depressed the most are:

• Comparing myself to others my age, I feel seriously behind, even when it comes down to my maturity. I'm just immature.

• I have zero friends, literally the last time I went out with a "Friend" was at least 2 years ago, when I was at college. Since leaving college I have not made 1 friend.

• When I'm in stressful situations, I have huge meltdowns I start rocking, covering my eyes and ears.

 • When I have something planned and I am looking forward to it, if it gets cancelled

or anything changes, I can **FLY** off the handle SOOO fast. I become spiteful and nasty.

• I rely on my parents for things people my age and younger shouldn't.

• I have issues with hygiene, (not in a bad way) just routines. Forgetting to brush my teeth or spray deodorant regularly.

• I have a **HUGE** phobia of bleach. I won't have cups or cutlery that I don't know where it has been or what it has been near. I get paranoid like someone has put bleach in my food or drink.

• My memory is incredible, I can recall strings of numbers like registration number plates, I only have to glance at it, and I can remember it.

• I'm extremely observant with people and patterns.

• I hate flashing lights.

• I hate noises or vibrating sounds or feelings that last a long time, like how a drill can make things vibrte; it cringes me out and I hate the thought of it not stopping.

• I want things my way or no way.

• I don't like routines (but I have noticed that there are routines that I do every day without realising.)

• I'm extremely obsessive.

• If I get into a Netflix series or whatever I have to binge watch it that day or night. I can't just watch one show a day. **NOOOO** I'll sit for 9 hours and not move a muscle.

• I don't like my food being cut in triangles!

• I hate socks.

• I hate anything going over my head, for example, dresses. If, they don't have a zip to undo or a button to loosen it when I take it off, I will have a full-on panic attack that I'm stuck.

• I hate and can't wear, clothes that feel tight, "itchy or scratchy" ... don't ask me to explain this, because I just can't.

• If I hear a rhyme or a sequence of music or something like knocking or humming, I have to do it or I just can't let it go. If I hear someone say a funny word, I have to repeat it otherwise it just gets louder in my mind.

• If someone makes a beat by knocking or banging, I have to copy it and I remember it for AGES. I just have to keep doing it as if it's a matter of life of death.

• Once I have an idea in my head there is no stopping me, I can't be told NO, otherwise I get angry and frustrated.

Things like those I have listed above are what affect me the most. Remember everybody has different  worries and struggles. When I told my doctor, we had a chat about how **PILLS DON'T TEACH YOU SKILLS**. She went on to explain that medication won't just magically make everything disappear overnight they help to suppress my symptoms and give me the confidence to get on with my daily life. I have to learn ways to cope and to adapt my life around my ADHD, as it's not going to be going anywhere.

## I'M STUCK WITH ADHD AND SO ARE YOU!

So, it's easier for us to try and get the positives out of it rather than just focusing on the bad things.
I was also told that what I'm still feeling and being affected by sounds a lot like autism or Asperger's syndrome. I have done my research since speaking to my doctor and I have never felt so strongly about something before. I have a feeling that I will get a diagnosis of Asperger's **OR** Autism. (So, everything that I'm writing is ADHD and maybe a little more). So, don't worry if you don't have all the same symptoms, we are all different and that's what makes us limited editions and unique. That being said, I have explored a lot of the conditions I listed above, and it all sounds **A LOT** like me. I don't know how many of these conditions I can actually have medically diagnosed but I don't think my journey of being diagnosed is anywhere near the end just **YET**.

Like I say everyone has their own journey and I'm just so happy you guys have decided to share mine.

It only gets crazier, once you read my personal experiences with school and college, I guarantee you will be able to relate to me.

# MY ADHD MAKES ME OBSESSIVE AND IMPULSIVE....

ADHD is like having a bag of crisps. They are all crisps but not one is the same shape or size as the other. Remember not everyone will suffer from the same difficulties and experiences, we are all different. But the **ONE** thing that makes us all a **FAMILY** is the superpowers we share and that is our ADHD.

I want to help others with ADHD. By telling you about **MY** most **ANNOYING** traits. Somethings just can't be fixed with medication. It can't take my most annoying traits away from me. **BUT** they make me who **I AM**. I wouldn't want to be **ME** without my superpower.

My impulsiveness is very dominant. It's very hard to control. I do things without thinking it through properly. Yes, being spontaneous is a great trait occasionally, but for me it's 10000X more intense; it can be my worst enemy. It can make things extremely stressful and challenging. Not only for me but for my family.

Being Impulsive has **ALWAYS** been a **HUGE** issue of mine.

My impulsiveness has been the instigator of **MANY** arguments at home. My impulsiveness has caused me  money troubles. I get myself into money troubles frequently. It doesn't only affect me, my parents have had to pay my debts for me because I don't have the money to pay them myself. It causes me a lot of inner anger and disappointment. It has also led to me having a complete emotional break down. It's a serious struggle for me. It is easily the **MOST** intense emotional trait I have. I can be happy one moment then I'm unfortunately reminded of something that I am impulsively **OBSESSED** with, and my moods flips almost instantaneously. Honestly, it happens as quickly and as easily as flicking a switch on and off.

I can go from being happy to an absolute volatile **MELTDOWN** in seconds. Because in my mind it feels like the world is obviously going to end. I become extremely frustrated and demanding; I even become aggressive. I can't seem to accept why I can't have it **NOW**. Then, just as quickly I calm down.

I demand to know **IF** I can get any loans, **THEN** if I can't, I need to know when I'll be able to afford it. There is absolutely nothing I can do. It's such a strong overwhelming feeling. I can't control it. I wish I could. But you know what, as I've gotten my diagnosis, I have been able to learn to accept that ADHD makes things harder but not impossible. I have learnt to try and just block out these impulsive outbursts by drawing or writing them down. It helps **ME**. It may help you - it might not, but don't worry you will find a mechanism that suits you best!

**PLEASE NEVER GIVE UP ...**

I'm going to tell you some more of my recklessness and impulsive behaviour because you aren't alone. I know it's hard, but we can get through this together trust me. Around about 3.5 years ago, I had not long passed my driving test and I was fortunate enough to have already bought myself a car. I borrowed the money from my grandad because I had seen a car and I wanted it. **OBVIOUSLY**, I had to get it that day. I couldn't stop thinking about it all day. I know it's natural to be excited but imagine being **OBSESSED WITH A CAR** to the point of getting angry and agitated. It started to cause tension at home so, my grandad reluctantly lent me the money so I would **SHUT UP**. I didn't sleep that night. I was up at the crack of dawn. Every minute was going by **SOOO SLOWLY**. It felt like I had been awake years when my grandad **FINALLY** turned up to take me to buy the car. There was nothing anyone could have told me that would have changed my mind. I wanted it so I **HAD** to get it, there was no other option in my mind. If I didn't get my way, there would be hell to pay. My parents were already scared of having to say **NO** to me. It wasn't a nice feeling learning just how much my behaviour affected my parents.

I look back now at the age of 21, and I strongly believe that me passing my driving test was one of the worst things that could have happened to me. Obviously not at that time, but it wasn't a very good idea, mixing my undiagnosed ADHD with independence and a car.

I was such a cocky driver. I had absolutely no Fear. I had no consideration for anyone else's safety. The scariest thing was not even my own safety concerned me. I would drive like an absolute lunatic. I wouldn't take any notice of, or care about the speed limits. I would go as fast as I wanted when I wanted. Yes, I know it wasn't right. Yes, I know I shouldn't have been driving but try telling me that at the time. I was unstoppable and out of control.

I will openly admit that I was a danger on the road. I had to give up driving as I was given a verbal warning by my black box insurance company for unsafe driving. I was driving over my annual mileage allowance monthly. I was racking up monthly bills that I couldn't afford, which put a **HUGE** financial burden on my parents. It got to the point where I couldn't afford it, and neither could my parents. It broke my heart that I had to sell my car.

And ever since that day I have been obsessed with cars. When I say obsessed, I mean to the point where I will sit and research them for hours. I would constantly be applying for finance and loans. These would all get rejected, which made things even more intense in my head. In my eyes. I couldn't see the impact I was having on my own mental health and those around me. In my eyes I was only trying to raise the money to get a car. If I didn't have a car, I wouldn't get the "friends" back that I had made the last time I had a car. I kept going on and on at my parents to lend me money, or to help me get a car in any way possible. It got to the point where it was causing **SOOO** much tension and **SOOO** many arguments at home.

When I FINALLY went and got diagnosed with ADHD, I was told that everything I had experienced above was actually down to my ADHD. Finally, I had the answer as to why I'm so **OBSESSIVE** and **IMPULSIVE** about things. Why I am **NOT** able to let things go and how having to have it **NOW** was actually **NORMAL** for **ME**.

I was also told that me being impulsive and obsessive is a typical **FEMALE** trait of ADHD.

This made so much sense to me. I wasn't a **FREAK**. I wasn't going to end up being a **PSYCHOPATH**. I had convinced myself that I was going to end up in prison. I just couldn't accept the fact that things don't just

happen when I want them all the time. I was worried it was going to end up with me doing something that would completely ruin my future for me. I was worried about me hurting myself or potentially someone else. But now I know that it's my ADHD.

My parents told me, shortly after starting my blog that they were always worried that they were going to receive a phone call about me either killing myself with my dangerous driving or killing someone else.

I didn't know I was that bad. However, now I look back at things I can see that I was dangerous and extremely selfish. I didn't take my own safety or anyone else into consideration.

I am currently not driving due to my ADHD **MEDICATION**, which is a good thing for me. As I personally feel like I still **DONT** have enough self-control. I wouldn't want to put anyone else at risk or myself.

Here are some other things I get over obsessive, compulsive, and impulsive about:

- **PEOPLE** - I have had a lot of trouble with being obsessed with people. Well, not exactly obsessed with them but just overly attached to them. I can't seem to let go of things. When I left school, I couldn't let go of some of the connections I had. For example, with one of my teachers. Not in a weird way, but I was so close to one of my teachers, I looked up to her like a "nan"

 figure. I have 1 grandparent, other than that I don't have any, and it has been like that since I was 7 years old. When I was able to speak to MRS M (the teacher) about my troubles and issues I finally felt like I had a

nan figure. Having lost my nan when I was only 7, I didn't have too many memories that I could actually remember very well. So, when she became my mentor, I was always with her. I grew up with having her by my side.

For 3 years, she was there when my parents were angry at me, she was there, and when I got myself into trouble outside of school on social media and other similar situations; I looked up to her like a "nan." That might sound strange or weird but honestly it wasn't, it was just a teacher- student relationship. But because I have ADHD I just became overly attached. When I left school, I felt as though I was grieving the loss (death) of another grandparent. I feel such intense strong connections.

This also comes with the fact not many people like me, and she gave me that attention I needed. It was as if my mum was there helping me through my anxiety at school. She inspired me to become the person I am today.

**EVERYONE WITH ADHD OR ANY BEHAVIOURAL OR EMOTIONAL CONDITION DESERVES A TEACHER LIKE MRS M. SHE WAS AN ABSOLUTE GEM. IT'S UNFORTUNATE NOT EVERYONE HAS A GREAT TEACHER LIKE HER. SCHOOL WOULD BE A MUCH BETTER AND SAFER PLACE IF WE COULD ALL BE BLESSED WITH A MRS M.**

- **MONEY** - To me having money means you are superior to others. Money makes my world go around for some reason.

- **NEW PHONES/GADGETS** - I have to have the latest version of the gadgets. I show them off to get attention. Those few days that people notice the "new phone" I am so happy. But once the novelty wears off, I'm thinking about the next purchase I can buy to show off.

• **MILESTONES** - I know they don't officially exist in adulthood. However, I have made my own list of milestones which I set myself mentally. Then, I am always hating myself for not reaching them. Things like having a boyfriend/a baby /a career at the same times my peers have them. It is like I convince myself that I am going to be a failure unless I meet them at that particular time of my life. I don't believe that I'm good enough for anything.

• **FRIENDSHIPS** - Friendships are very hard for me. I seem to just not know how to be someone's friend. I always ruin it. Not intentionally, but because I'm trying too **HARD** to keep them as my friend; I become overpowering and bossy. I'm just not very good at social situations and relationships. I struggle with my ADHD symptoms and my anxiety disorder. It all plays a part in my failed friendships. I get paranoid that I have upset them if they don't speak to me 24/7. If they have other friends, I become nasty and spiteful because I don't like knowing or feeling I could be replaced. I always have to have that reassurance **CONSTANTLY**. I always call them **MY BEST FRIEND.**

**IT'S HARD FOR ME TO JUST BE MYSELF AROUND OTHERS**.

• **SIBLING JEALOUSY** - I can become a nasty person within seconds. I'm well aware my sister is going to achieve extraordinary things in her lifetime, there's no doubt about it. There is also no hiding the fact that I am so incredibly proud of everything she has achieved ... and what she is going to achieve. She will rock this world but sometimes it's very difficult for me to accept that she is going to be successful. I know I have challenges, but I just don't want to look like a disappointment compared to her. I become obsessed in a competitive way. I don't mean to; I know that my sister feels like she can't talk to me about things like her dreams or her achievements, as I have to turn it around to me. I just can't seem to handle the fact she is smashing it and I'm still struggling to work a part time job for only 5 hours, four days a week. I feel inadequate and a disappointment. I become very upset with myself and it turns our sister bond toxic and that hurts me.

- **JEALOUSLY** - If I see someone I know or that I knew, with a boyfriend, or a car, or whatever it is I become depressed and obsessed that I don't have a boyfriend, or that nice car. In my mind if I have all these material things. I will make friends just to look like I have my life together. I really hope these help parents or even those with ADHD themselves understand that it's normal. We can't help it. It's like our brains are programmed to be this way, and the more we accept it, the easier it becomes to make positive changes to help ourselves or others with ADHD. Accepting that there is a problem is the hardest thing to do. But believe me, when you do, it helps others around you to understand that you can't help it. That, what you're going through is actually more frustrating for the person going through it, rather than the people who have to just listen to them going **ON AND ON** ... Honestly, it's a hidden talent to be able to be spontaneous and impulsive. It can even be a blessing at times.

Don't ask me when, because I'm personally still trying to figure that one out, but I'm told that there are positives to our crazy traits!

CARRY ON READING YOU'LL BE EVEN MORE SURPRISED TO KNOW THAT YOU AREN'T ACTUALLY ALONE AFTER ALL. YOU HAVE ME!

# MY ANXIETY AND HOW IT ALL STARTED FOR ME

## What are my triggers?

Just remember not everyone will have anxiety about the same things I do … Everyone is different.

Anxiety has always been a **HUGE** part of my life for as far back as I can remember. I have vivid memories of having anxiety attacks, when I was young about being separated from my mum. I hated being apart from my mum. She is and always will be my best friend. She is the only one I feel comfortable around, and she is the only one who understands me and takes the time to truly listen to me. My mum has the most caring heart, and she is the only one who can help me whenever I have a really bad panic attack. I feel safe with her around. I wouldn't be able to cope without my mum.

I can remember one time when I was a lot younger about 10 or 11 years old. One evening my mum went out with one of her friends and I stayed at home with my dad and younger sister. I wouldn't settle, and I couldn't go to sleep, because I thought that she wouldn't be coming back. I have always been heavily dependent on my mum … for everything! The only person who can reassure me is my mum. The only person that has ever given me the friendship,  emotional support, and guidance I need is my **MUM**. I remember one evening my god-mother Sally was babysitting me, and the song that I associated my mum with came on the tv, all my emotions came at me **FAST**.

I became over- emotionally sensitive, my separation anxiety also played up and I could **NOT** control any of it. This has always been and always will be a major problem, although these days, it isn't as overwhelming as it was when I was younger. I still can't complete a shift at work without texting my mum or having a meltdown … or a panic attack. She has and is, as always there to calm me down. I may be 21 but I still need my mum just as much, or possibly even more than ever now.

I have always had a sleeping problem. I can't sleep in my own room; I have always had to sleep in my mum and dad's bedroom. When I was a lot younger my parents took me to see a sleep therapist. She told us that it was obvious I had a kind of sleep anxiety.

**SOMETHING THAT I THINK CAN HELP OTHER PARENTS THAT DEAL WITH THIS IS …**

The sleep therapist told my parents that if it's not hurting me or them **WHAT IS THE PROBLEM?**

I went through a stage where it got better. I was able to sleep in my own room, but it has gone downhill rapidly the past 5/6 years. This is a **HUGE** step for me to admit this, but I'm currently unable to sleep in my own room. I'm having to sleep on my parents' floor. This is something I find extremely hard and very embarrassing to admit to anyone, although to be honest, I don't even understand it myself. I just get some comfort from sleeping in the same room as my mum. I feel safer and more content. If I sleep in a separate room, I can't sleep at all; I have anxiety attacks, my legs and hands go numb, and I just can't seem to settle.

Emotions
Anxiety
ADHD
Critism
Some pills
Are harder
to swallo

# MY BIGGEST FEAR CAME TRUE

My career goal was to become a military police dog handler. It has **ALWAYS** been my dream. I was sooo focused on becoming the policewoman I had always wanted to be, but when I was diagnosed with ADHD, it all came crashing down. It broke my **HEART**. I thought that my life was over. I have **NEVER** wanted any other job ... I have never wanted anything as **MUCH** as I wanted to be a policewoman. I was devastated. I had worked so hard towards it. I felt like it was the only thing that I wanted, and that I would be good at. I can't do anything else. I'm not good enough for anything academic.

That last paragraph was **VERY** relevant to my journey with anxiety.

When I was younger, I was enrolled into the "Army cadets." I was so proud that I was a part of it, I finally felt like I had a chance at becoming more than that **NAUGHTY KID AT SCHOOL**. I was determined to get my dream career!

I was about 13, and this was a specific day - Remembrance Day. I was on parade with the army cadets. I was so proud **OF MYSELF**. Most importantly all my family were there to watch me do my first parade with the cadets. But little did I know that this particular day was the last time I would ever feel "Normal." To this day even speaking about it brings tears to my eyes. It breaks my heart completely. It ruined my whole life, and I won't ever forget it. I was stood on parade, listening to the veterans speak about their experiences and how they got through the war. When, all of a sudden, the girl I was stood next to fainted. I was obviously shocked and a little concerned, but I managed to justify it by assuming that she probably hadn't eaten anything yet (we were told that you had to eat breakfast before standing on parade or fainting could potentially happen). So, after that I just zoned out and carried on smiling to myself and continued thinking how proud my nan would have been, and how proud my parents were of me. Then, the boy standing in front of me fell backwards into me; he had also fainted, and I can remember feeling this weird sensation take over my whole body. It had never happened to me before. I could feel my heart beating in my chest and even in the back of my throat; everything just went numb and tingly. I can remember looking at my mum in complete fear, I had never felt the way that I did right then. It was a new experience for me!

**BUT LITTLE DID YOUNG MOLLY KNOW, SHE WAS HAVING A PANIC ATTACK, THE FIRST OF MILLIONS I HAVE HAD SINCE THEN.**

My mum took me to the first aid room. I was convinced I was going to faint or something bad was about to happen to me. As soon as I felt my mums hug it went away, almost instantly. I felt safe and secure. I went back out on parade thinking it was over and done with, but **OH NO!!** That same feeling came back with a  vengeance and this time it took over my whole body. I have never felt anything so strong in my life. It felt like I was being possessed. I had no control of how I was feeling, and I ran back to the safety of my mum.

From this day onward I have had a toxic relationship with **MY** anxiety. It is something I can honestly say has control of me. It doesn't matter what tablets I'm put on it is always there. It's a demon! It has ruined my childhood/teens and it certainly hasn't made my adulthood any easier that's for sure. It's a part of me now. It's like my evil twin, but without it I wouldn't be me.

I could never go back to army cadets; I tried a few times, **BUT** every time I was stood on parade that horrible sensation came back and took control of me again. So, I sadly gave up army cadets.

This is when my behaviour and anxiety were at their worst, I felt as if I had no purpose, and my anxiety was coming out as bad behaviour. It was a time in my life where I was the most misunderstood kid. I had never felt so alone. I was trying to understand my mind and trying to control it, but it just wasn't working for me. This was a bad time for young undiagnosed Molly. I was hiding the fact I was struggling with bad behaviour; it was my minds escapism.

If I was to rate my anxiety on a scale of 1-10, I would say it's a good 9.5. It is all based around my health, more specifically my **EYES, EARS**, and **JAW**. I worry tremendously about those things. I also worry a lot about what others think of me, what my future is going to entail, what if I don't ever get a boyfriend, and why aren't I like other people; my mind is never at ease. It's constantly in overdrive, resulting in extreme mental exhaustion or anger and frustration. I have tried counselling, I have spoken to GP's, I've been at rock bottom but honestly the only thing that gets me through any of it is my MUM! When my mum hugs me it's as if an angel has come down to earth and is giving me the love and guidance and that I need.

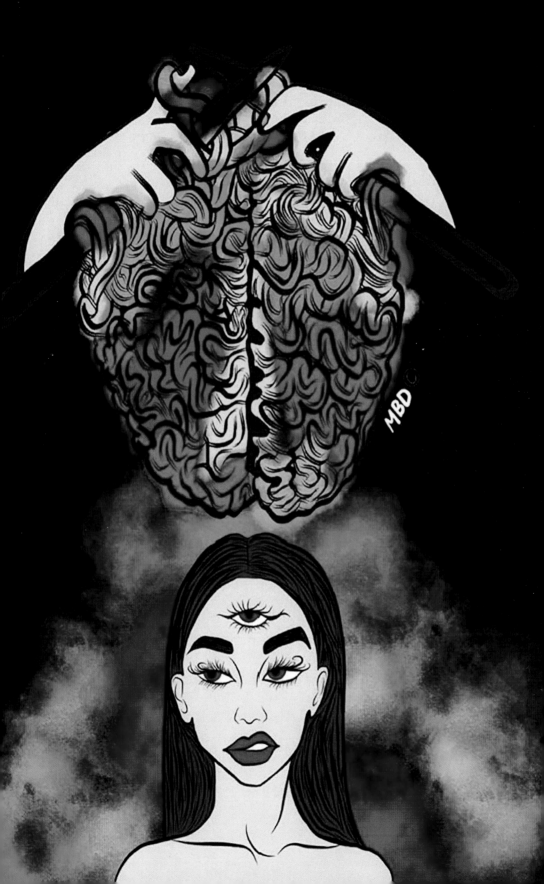

# My survival Tips to get MYSELF through my anxiety attacks:

**They might help you to get through a bad panic attack. I hope they help. I try to take my mind off my anxiety by:**

- Watching YouTube
- Watching Netflix
- Speaking to someone you trust
- Learning breathing techniques
- Trying to close my eyes and focus on my heartbeat; just breathe
- Learning to work out what *your* triggers are
- Setting realistic goals that are achievable like Exercise or walking the dog? Or just going for a walk in general.
- Trying to find an active hobby to focus on, for example mine is photography and when I'm anxious I love to go out and take photos. Write things in a book or make a blog!!!

Remember though, it doesn't matter what Gender you are, how old you are or how you think you should be feeling. If you need help don't need to be afraid or worried about what others might think of you. It is not a sign of weakness asking for help. Speaking to someone helps. Everyone experiences some form of anxiety but when you have to live with it every day it  starts to get you down. I know that feeling all too well, and the best thing I did was talk to my mum about how I was feeling. You can get the support and help you need just ask for it. **You got this!!!!!**

# MY ANXIETY

I want to try explaining to you what my anxiety feels like, so others can understand that having anxiety isn't a weakness. Also, I want my readers without ADHD to have a better understanding of what others with ADHD go through. We have ADHD which can have traits like impulsiveness and hyperactivity. These can lead to Hyper focusing on our anxiety and stress. We can't just stop thinking about things, it's not as easy as that for us. As soon as we stop thinking about that particular thing, our mind starts overthinking about something else.

Anxiety is still is my **BIGGEST FIGHT**. Every day, I worry about a variety of different things such as:

•     **My weight** - I have become obsessed with my weight. I have begun being very cautious about what I eat, and I stop myself enjoying food. I always feel guilty about eating a "Treat" as I don't want to put weight on. I get really obsessed with the numbers on the scale.

•     **Not having any friends** - This has been a major worry for me. Making friends is **VERY** hard for me. I always worry that I'm going to be alone and not ever find one friend. I dread and hate my birthday as I haven't ever received a card from a "Friend." I always try to convince myself it's going to be **OK** …
I tell myself that I'll find a friend one day, but every birthday or Christmas it gets harder. Also, when I see my younger sister having friends and going out it gets even **HARDER**.

It breaks my heart more every single time. I just want to be "**NORMAL**" and I long for that perfect friendship, but it just hasn't ever happened for me.

- **I worry about my future A LOT**. I worry about what career I am going to end up with. I worry that my future isn't going to be as good as my sisters or cousins, or that I will be the family disappointment.

- **I worry that I won't have the chance** to have a relationship and have children and live the life I so desperately desire.

- **I worry about not meeting 'milestones'** - that other people, my age are accomplishing. For example, having kids, getting engaged, going to UNI. I always feel like I am failing and I'm behind, which makes me feel really jealous which comes out as anger and depression. This even happens when my younger sister achieves something that I haven't. I get to the point where I wear myself out and end up knocking my own confidence down; because I have built this perfect life in my head that I think I need to be living in order to be successful. I know me though, and just getting through a 5-hour work shift is a **HUGE** success for me.

**I have learnt to try (which is hard) and think about the positives in my life NOW, and not think too much about the future.**

**My biggest Phobia, fear and anxiety is anything based around My own personal health.** It gets

obsessive to the point that if someone is near me in a wheelchair or in the doctors, I will physically hold my breath because I'm so paranoid that I'm going to contract some type of illness.

**My worst fear is getting a brain tumour.** Most people worry about this I know, but it's on my mind constantly. If I get a headache, I will have convinced myself I have a brain tumour by the end of the day.

Alongside that I also have a **HUGE** fear of something happening to my eyes. This has stopped me going to work or going out in general. This is a Trigger for my anxiety and 9 times out of 10, it is the thing that triggers my **BAD** panic attacks. This can lead to me hurting myself either mentally or physically out of pure stress and emotion; just being petrified. I will **PUNCH** myself really hard in the head or pinch my legs and arms. It's really hard to cope with, and these days I have a dog which helps me to cope.

**Another thing that affects me with my ADHD, is my impulsiveness.** This has caused **A LOT** of stress and upset. I have literally signed myself up for about 10 different car finance loans. I spend impulsively, like buying expensive shoes when I can't afford them, or when I don't need them, as I already have them in 2 or 3 different colours. I don't care at the time I still buy them. Then **SLOWLY** I begin regretting it, usually when I look at my bank statement and realise that I can't afford my mobile phone bill. I have got better since being on medication, as being medicated gives me a bit more time to evaluate the situation. Then I decide if I genuinely need them, or if I can actually afford to pay the loans or credit cards back.

**Overall ADHD has made my life extremely difficult but far from boring.** There are things that I have done that still make me laugh now. I enjoyed my school life, but I did things that **OBVIOUSLY** I shouldn't have although I was never out to hurt anyone intentionally. I just wanted to fit in and have that feeling of being liked and having an actual friend … that liked me. I just wanted others to like me as much as I needed them to.

I've met some incredible Teachers/mentors along my way through education. There were two amazing women that both made a huge impact on me. I wouldn't be the person I am today without their mentoring and guidance. They made me believe that I deserved better than I was allowing myself to achieve. They taught me that not everyone will give up on me or let me down. There were many times that I could have been permanently excluded. **BUT** those two **ANGELS** had my back and **GOT ME THROUGH**. I left school with minimal GCSES, but I did it.

This is Mrs M and Mrs C

Mrs C

Mrs M

It was a journey and a half, but I tell you what, I would have been super lucky to have had even **ONE** teacher, that actually had my back. They made things so much easier for me.

I could be feeling so anxious and worried but to the other teachers I was potentially trying to be disruptive (I wasn't *always* doing it purposely), **BUT** these two teachers **JUST KNEW** that it was my way of **HIDING** that I was struggling.

I was never really able to tell them just how much I appreciated them. Losing my nan at a young age was hard, but these two ladies were just what I needed to help, guide, and support me: someone other than just my mum and dad. One was like a "Nanny" Figure, the other one was like a strict "Mother" figure and I needed both to help me become the **MOLLY** I am today.

Throughout all of this, I feel so sorry for my parents and my younger sister. They had to put up with so much abuse and hatred from me. **THEY WERE ALL AMAZING!!** They still love me and have my back even after all of that! But even after putting my family through **HELL**, I still feel **EXTREMELY** sorry for the **YOUNGER** Molly.

I was alone in my Little brain, in a world that was **SOOOO** scary. I was just living like it was normal, I had no way of knowing anything different. It was normal to me, to be unable to voice my concerns. I just thought I was the girl no one liked because I was weird and ugly. I didn't want to be nasty to my family, I didn't want to ruin my career, or my future self. I was just **MISUNDERSTOOD**.

ADHD really deserves to be understood in order to be accepted by others. The whole world seems to believe it's just an excuse to cause mayhem. But nothing is worth the self-disappointment we go through for it to be that simple. All we need is a little support love, acceptance, and time. We really are going to conquer the world one day. We are just as intelligent as anyone else; we just have a little **TWIST** and some extra ingredients tomake us extra spicy.

**Along with my anxiety I have some pretty intense phobias and fears.**

I'm, not sure why it all started or what was the cause of these phobias; it's just one of my many quirks that I have in my daily life. So here it is, since about 11or 12 years old I have had a phobia of drinking out of cups/eating food from a plate/cutlery /food in general that I don't know where it was prepared, or if it has been near any bleach.

I have had many therapy sessions for my phobias, both at school and outside with my anxiety therapy. I have tried helping myself, by doing things like making sure I clean my own cups and utensils. I physically can't leave a drink in the kitchen and go back to it in a couple of minutes just in case someone has put bleach in my drink. Even though I know that no one would ever do that to me. Going into the kitchen itself is like my own personal version of **HELL**. There are so many different kitchen cleaning sprays that I have phobias of, but **BLEACH** is my biggest fear. The fear of it going into my eyes, or anywhere near my skin causes me absolute **TERROR**.

Im petrified that someone is going to throw bleach or acid into my face or eyes when I'm walking along the street. It's one of those things: you can have as many cognitive therapy sessions as you like, but it won't go away. It's as if it's imprinted into my brain. If I wasn't scared of bleach, and I heard that someone else was I would have laughed at them. It's such a peculiar thing to be scared of but what about me is normal anyway and what even, is normal?

It got so bad that I was buying 2 or 3 toothbrushes a week because I was paranoid that someone had dipped my toothbrush in the "toilet cleaning bleach" ... it is a genuine and terrifying fear of mine.

As I've grown up it has got better to some extent, but it still affects me every day; going out to eat is a nightmare for me. I worry that they haven't cleaned the cutlery or drinking glasses properly, or that they haven't rinsed the cleaning products off correctly. I'm scared it's going to go into my mouth, or that someone will purposely try to poison me.

**Some other things I DON'T like:**

- My hands being sticky.
- My clothes being too tight or too clingy.
- Food in the shape of triangles.
- Socks.
- Jewellery.
- Bright lights.
- Loud noises.
- Eye contact.
- Anything health related (symptoms or germs).

It is very difficult for others to understand how much ADHD can affect us and to **HIGHLIGHT** the phobias us, ADHD **SUFFERERS** have. Where I suffer from the combined type of ADHD, I find my symptoms really intense at times. I can't just stop thinking about things. It gets really intense and **REALLY LOUD**. I can't seem to just calm down and think reasonably.

# WHAT IS IT LIKE TO HAVE S.A.D

I'm going to try and explain what is going on inside the mind of someone suffering from S.A.D, by explaining my own personal experiences; just how and what my S.A.D condition feels like to me.

## What does S.A.D mean?

S ... SOCIAL

A ... ANXIETY

D ... DISORDER

I want to tell others how it feels to have S.A.D (Social anxiety Disorder). It can be a scary place when you have to deal with it alone. If you are suffering from this, please speak to someone. And, if you know someone else who is suffering from this please reach out to them and offer them support.

I have found out new things about myself. Well not **NEW** things, but things I have always tried to brush aside or ignore. I would have just branded myself a "freak" for simply not enjoying social situations. When I was diagnosed with ADHD I was also officially diagnosed with SAD and generalised anxiety. It wasn't  a surprise to me or something I didn't already know – I knew that I had anxiety. The social anxiety part was something I wasn't fully aware of or even understood.

**When I was younger, I DON'T remember suffering from social anxiety at all.**

I **ALWAYS** wanted to be the centre of attention at school and in social situations. It just wasn't as big of an issue for me then as it is now. I used to shout and scream in the corridors. I used to walk out of lessons and assembly's in front of loads of people without any hesitation or anxiety at all. I used to say what I wanted, and I didn't care about anyone else's opinions or feelings. I used to do what I wanted, when I wanted, and had fun doing it. I would talk to whoever I wanted, whenever I wanted without thinking twice about it.

But now I over think **every** situation. I can't do anything without having to think through all the potentially dangerous situations; how long it will take me to get home if something bad happens to me or my family. I seem to always end up, winding myself up with crazy scenarios that have a 2% (probably 0%) chance of ever happening to me.

I basically never leave the house; I just like being in my own house. I can't do things on my own, and I love being with my mum as she makes me feel calm and safe, but there are some situations, in which that isn't even enough to help me. I hate being away from her. I never feel safe without her. Everyone else just doesn't understand me. I feel like I'm being a pest with anyone else.

**Situations I find hard:**

- Going shopping.

- Going to appointments.

• Being alone with a person. I feel pressured to start conversations and I find myself talking about rubbish.

• When people try to make eye contact with me. Overly confident people make me just want to run away and hide.

• Gym / swimming pools.

• Going up to the tills at shops and having to pay, I check my online balance, and my cash is counted multiple times and I get others to check it as well before I go to pay.

• Speaking to anyone that I don't feel completely comfortable around; I end up stressing and panicking.

• Bright lights and loud noises.

• I have to take my mum with me everywhere: dentist appointments, doctor's appointments, hairdresser appointments. I also get my mum to speak for me.

• My dad does all of my phone communication, as I can't speak to people over the phone.

• I'm self-conscious in front of other people.

• I'm extremely afraid that others will judge me.

• I can worry for days, or weeks before an event.

• I avoid situations that require social

interaction and I am intensely uncomfortable in any social situation.

• I have difficulty talking so others so, I keep conversation with others to a minimum.

• I have difficulty making or keeping friends.

• I suffer from panic attacks, including shaking, blushing, nausea, or sweating, when in a social situation.

• I strongly dislike being around others I don't know. I worry they are going to judge me or be nasty towards me. I would much prefer to be in my room with puppy, watching YouTube or drawing or writing. I don't know how to act around other people I always feel as if I will embarrass myself or my family in-front of others.

I **ALWAYS** worry that I look fat or ugly. I get very paranoid, so I stick to wearing the same baggy clothes. I own about 8 hoodies in extra big sizes; I sit with my hood up. I don't feel good enough. I always fear that others will judge me or say something that will hurt me. It's like I'm waiting to hear something bad about myself, so I am constantly trying to listen in order to hear someone say something about me.

I post stuff on social media to "get likes." It makes me feel more popular if I get more than my average amount of likes on my post. If I don't get any likes, my heart literally breaks, and I feel worthless. Social media plays a massive part in my anxiety. I recently made the decision to delete some social media accounts in order to give myself a **BREAK**. It has honestly done me the world of good.

In social situations I never feel like I'm truly welcome. Recently I've been in situations where I have been speaking to a few people. They were complementing me and my work. I couldn't help thinking that really, they wanted me to leave. I couldn't help myself and made up an excuse to leave; I needed to leave to meet "someone." In truth, I just wanted to get out of yet another situation where my brain was telling me that I'm not good enough and people don't really want me there.

It's hard making friends or even keeping them for that matter. I convince myself that I'm easily replaced and that I'm not worthy of a meaningful friendship. I hate that social anxiety is so hard for me handle. It's like a really fast merry-go-round spinning in my head, that makes the walls cave-in and the floor feel as though it is sucking you in. It's a horrible feeling when you feel as if you are sinking and being told that you aren't really welcome there. It's hard to deal with sometimes, which is why I enjoy my own company instead of being in a group.

I'm easily intimidated, I never understand other people's intentions or social expectations. I think I will always have this issue. I'm just trying to not let it ruin or take over my life. Having support can really help make it easier.

Keep smiling.
Keep talking, but most importantly …
Keep being YOU!!!

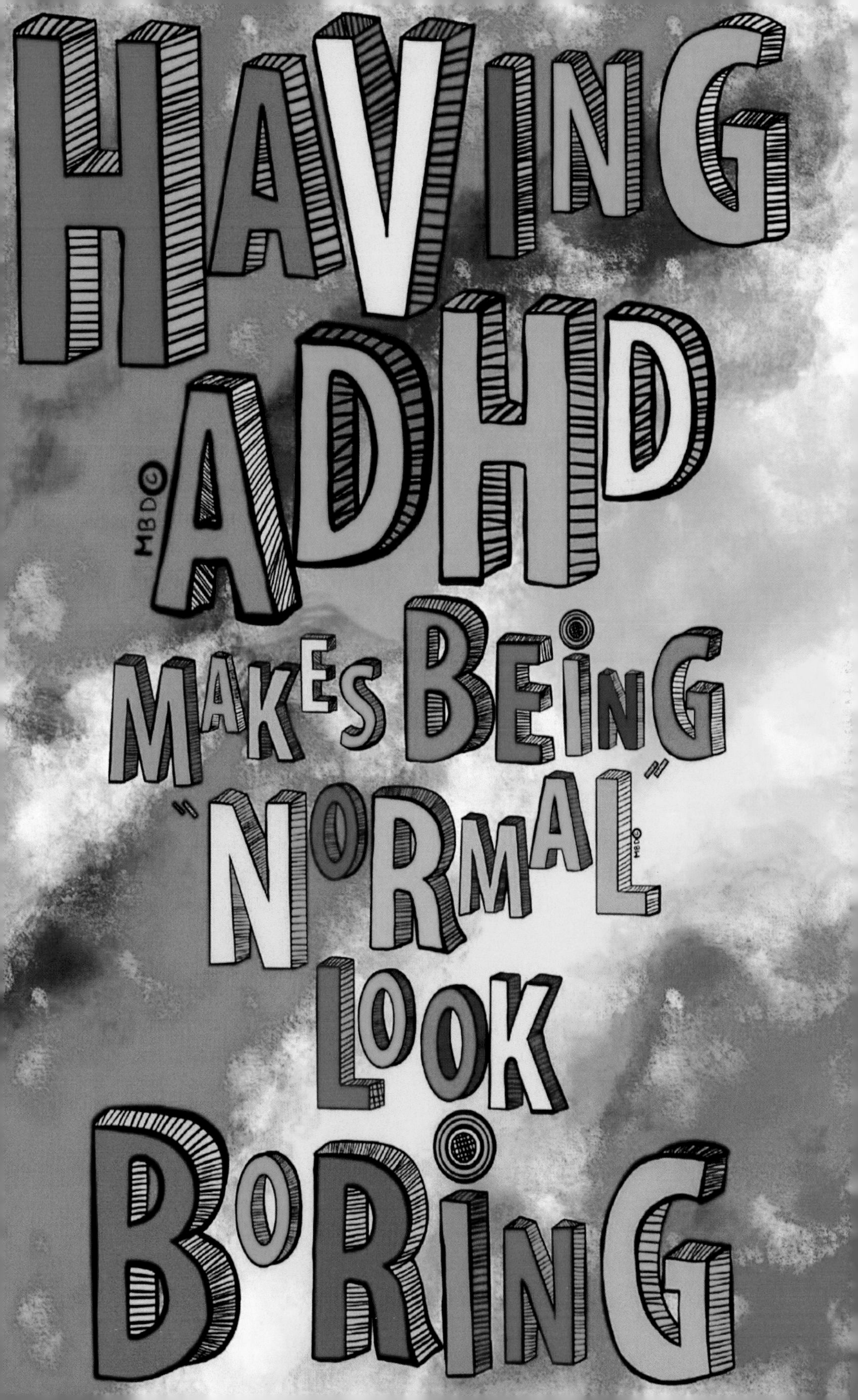
HAVING
ADHD
MAKES BEING
"NORMAL"
LOOK
BORING
MBD©

# ANGER AND ADHD

When I think about my ADHD the hardest thing to cope with is the fact that you aren't the only one who suffers from ADHD; the people you love also suffer at the hands of your ADHD. The meltdowns, the physical and verbal abuse, the exhaustion of constantly worrying what's going to happen next: constantly stressed and anxious. So, when I think about my ADHD, I just feel so guilty, and upset, I hate what I have put my family through. The hardest part of it all, is that my family only ever try to love and support me, and I can be so unlikable at times, but, even so, they have never stopped loving me and being by my side.

Even though people suffer physically and mentally from my ADHD, I still can't tell my brain not to have a meltdown; I can't control my actions when I'm in one of my moods. There is no excuse in the world that can justify being disrespectful to your family, but one thing I want you to know is that we don't mean any of it ... **NOT ONE WORD!**

In a weird way you should feel privileged knowing that we can openly express our emotions around you. We sometimes have to suppress all our anxieties, emotions, and frustrations in order to disguise our vulnerabilities. This can lead to huge melt downs or  panic attacks when we finally feel safe enough to let our emotions explode. We usually only allow our guards down when we are with those we love and feel safe around.

My anger and anxiety had caused devastating consequences for my family and I'm sure that it's not just mine. I subjected my family to heart-breaking realities, making life extremely difficult and sometimes uncomfortable for those around me. Thankfully, I have an amazing family, they all support me. They never wanted me to feel like it was my fault. Well let's just put it this way; I can go from being **SUPER CALM** to **VERY VOLATILE** and to **MEGA-ANGRY** faster than you can say **ADHD!**

It must have been exceptionally difficult for my family to have to put up with that 24/7. It certainly caused many arguments and I ended up pushing away the ones I love the most.

It's actually very hard to deal with at times, obviously we have absolutely no control over this, and there are times when I get myself so worked up over something, that the only way my brain knows how to deal with it all is by taking it out on someone who won't judge me and who actually cares. I don't mean to, I just have trouble regulating my feelings, understanding how I can act appropriately. This can be so intense at times. I can't let things go; I agonise over them until my head goes **BANG!!!!** I'm not a confrontational person at all. The last thing **ANY OF US** want is to hurt someone. It's almost like I have an evil twin inside me, who likes to come out occasionally to spice things up a bit and make things a little more unpredictable. I've been told before that I'm like Jekyll and Hyde, one moment I'm sweet and content and then all of a sudden, I'm furious and evil. I've also been called Tigger from Winnie the Pooh: Hyper, bouncy, springy, and constantly on the go.

I have been known to ruin family days out over my anger issues. If I don't get my own way, it just sets off my inner ferociousness. I get very aggressive and aggravated. My moods get very intense and it's almost like I'm not happy until I've hurt someone's feelings or ruined the day completely. Eventually I finally snap out of my Jekyll and Hyde moments and I am absolutely devastated and embarrassed. I never want to make someone feel bad. I hate this part of ADHD because it is the most intense and unnecessary part of ADHD.

I'm not at all proud of this but I want to be as honest, open, and transparent with you as I can. I have physically hurt my dad multiple times, due to my anger building up so much that I can't just physically shout as it's not enough so, I have to lash out. I have physically hurt myself and others. Sometimes it's just throwing something, but it has been worse before. I'm not proud of this at all, I don't want people thinking I condone this behaviour I certainly **DO NOT!!!** But this is part of my story and I want to share it, so others know that we aren't vicious or vindictive people all the time. We just have absolutely no control over how quickly we are triggered.

When we get angry, we almost turn into gorillas. They are known to be a very social and intelligent animal most of the time, who are capable of deceiving even the greatest of animals. But, when they feel under threat, they become very dominant animals who don't always mix well with other animals. When they are angry, they  are **ANGRY!!!**, they use their powerful fists to destroy everything and everyone in their paths: they are usually humble and nurturing but when they feel threatened, they can't help but protect their feelings and anxiety from others. They have to hide their weaknesses by covering them up and lashing out. Once, it blows over, they turn back into the cheeky monkeys they truly are. Happy, loving, playful and needy.

When you love someone with ADHD, you learn that they aren't taking it out on you deliberately or victimising you. It's simply, because they feel safe and are able to show their emotions around you; comfortable enough to share their true feelings. We are not Horrible. We just have to learn to **THINK BEFORE WE SPEAK**. I'm 21 and trust me, I still haven't got a clue how to handle my anger. I am like a sponge. I absorb all my feelings and then I get too heavy and they need to be squeezed out of me!

On behalf of all of us ADHD warriors, we want our families and friends to know that we love you, we might not show it but seriously, without you we wouldn't have a clue how to cope. You guys are like the glue that holds us adhders together. We are fragile human beings that just need to feel loved and contented. We don't have many people that are willing to love us with all of our flaws like you do, but we can't always help how we act. We just feel safe around you and we know you won't judge us. Thank you for always being there for us when things get too much. Thank you for loving us even when it's almost impossible. But Thank you from the bottom of our hearts for accepting us and being our support system!

You parents and carers, or partners that deal with us daily are incredibly strong people! I don't know how you cope! But you are like soldiers, you get straight back up

again, and you face it like a **BOSS!** You guys are the real heroes! You don't get enough credit!

But just remember, we don't mean the horrible things we say! We truly appreciate you, for having our best interests at heart! We will forever be thankful and forever need you by our sides.

# HOW THE SYMPTOMS OF ADHD DIFFER BETWEEN MALE AND FEMALES?

So, like you guys know, I'm far from a professional but since being diagnosed I have done **A LOT** of hyper focusing research. **HOWEVER,** including me, there are not a lot of people who know that ADHD affects genders differently, and in fact, it couldn't affect them more differently.

I have been at the receiving end of the stigma attached to "Girls not being able to suffer from ADHD." I was always told it was because my anxiety was **BAD**, and that was what was making me feel so angry and isolated all the time. When I was at school, I was made out to be the "naughty kid" who intentionally had an 'attitude problem?" Or that I was just trying to be difficult.

I look back now, and I feel so sorry for my younger self. I was so obviously struggling and showing the signs of ADHD. Like I said previously my parents had chosen not to get me diagnosed when I was younger. I made the decision to get myself tested when I was 18. It took $2^{1/2}$ years, but it definitely explained **A LOT** of my differences. I know that ADHD isn't a well-known disorder and it still has the stigma that it is a made-up illness. Most adults believe that it is just an excuse for children to get away with "naughty" behaviour.

I personally have suffered with **BAD** anxiety and self-esteem issues. When I was at school, I was very misunderstood. I never knew how to control my emotions, but most importantly I didn't know I was acting differently to the other children. It wasn't, until about year 9 that it became apparent to **A LOT** of people who were around me regularly that there was something not quite right with me. I kept walking out of lessons and answering back. I look back now and can see that I was obviously struggling, and I was trying to cover up the fact I was struggling academically.

I naturally assigned myself the role of class clown **ALWAYS**. I was clearly covering up the fact that I didn't ever fit in, and that I didn't know how to make friends. I would try to belittle others or be nasty to others to try and make myself feel superior to them.

I wouldn't get changed for PE because I was so embarrassed about my body and I couldn't dare let anyone know my insecurities. I just had to hide the fact I was **STRUGGLING**. I would be **OVERPOWERING** and loud to cover up the noise inside my head. The noise was of me screaming on the inside. I was seriously crying out for help, but I was screaming for help silently in my own head.

I craved the attention to make it feel like I actually had some friends. I was just so lonely and struggling. I was taking it out on others and myself because I didn't know what was wrong with me. I wasn't diagnosed until I was 21. I still struggle to this day with body issues and anxiety, but thankfully I have my amazing family and the community support which I have built up on my blog page really has helped me. This is why I want to offer my experiences and emotions to help you realise that you aren't alone!

This book is like a personal diary of my own experiences and it's also intended to help parents, teachers, and carers of someone with ADHD. I never want anyone else, to feel like I did, growing up. This is to help you guys understand those people with ADHD, and some of its effects.

Us girls, seem to slip through the radar a lot more. Girls with ADHD usually show more of the inattentive symptoms of ADHD, whereas boys usually show more of the hyperactive symptoms (obviously this isn't **ALWAYS** the case). Male ADHD is a lot easier to spot when looking for the obvious and main symptoms of ADHD; the hyperactivity which is more dominant in males than in Females (again not always). Boys seem to be a lot easier to identify as ADHD sufferers/ survivors.

Girls/women with ADHD are more prone to eating disorders, self-esteem, depression, and anxiety disorders. This is because females are more likely to be affected by the need to be accepted in society. Women are more well-known for camouflaging their behaviours and emotions to fit in with their friends or family.

This is why it often ends up becoming more of an issue for women/girls having compulsive disorders and self-esteem issues which lead to poor mental health and body images. The male symptoms usually show more when they are at home or in the classroom or in their workplace environments.

- This maybe because the person can't sit still or concentrate.

•     They may behave in an impulsive or dangerous manner that is more apparent than in girls with ADHD.

•     The inattentive behaviours are often less visible in boys than they are with girls.

I'm not saying either gender has it worse than the other one. It's just a fact that I found interesting and I believe that others will also find it interesting.

Not a lot of parents or teachers know that ADHD can affect genders differently, so, I thought I would do my best to explain some of this, with the knowledge I have. Girls with ADHD don't usually show the "typical" signs of ADHD. The symptoms aren't usually as obvious in girls than they are in boys. Females symptoms are usually more "hidden" or "invisible." They don't always show the most "stereotypical" symptoms as much as a Males:

They could include:

•     Being withdrawn
•     Low self-esteem
•     Anxiety
•     Intellectual impairment
•     Difficulty with academic achievement
•     Inattentiveness or a tendency to "daydream"
•     Trouble focusing
•     Appearing not to listen
        •     Verbal aggression, such as teasing, taunting, or name-calling
        •     Talking excessively
        •     Frequently interrupting other people's coversations and activities.

Males with ADHD tend to show the symptoms that are mostly "stereotyped" with ADHD behaviour.

They could include:

• Impulsivity or "acting out"

• Hyperactivity, such as running, hitting, and constantly getting up and moving around.

• Lack of focus and concentration

• They struggle to sit still and relax

• Physical aggression

• Fighting or getting in trouble with the police a lot more than girls with ADHD do.

This is why boys are nearly three times more likely to be diagnosed with ADHD than girls. This is because male symptoms are a lot more visible compared to the female symptoms which are usually happening inside their minds. These include anxiety, depression, and self-esteem issues which are less visible. Girls get diagnosed, on average **FIVE YEARS** later than males.

Even though ADHD is more often under-diagnosed in girls it can be missed in boys just as much. Boys are typically seen as being overly energetic and hyper, so when they run around and act out, it usually gets put down as "boys being boys." but when they start suffering academically it also gets put down to them trying to be "the class clown." So, both genders have their troubles when it comes to being diagnosed but the symptoms differ from gender to gender.

Basically, my whole reason for writing this was to raise the awareness that just because females don't show the same symptoms that males do, it doesn't mean that either of the genders have it worse. It just means they can affect each individual differently. What affects me may not affect another woman/girl but could quite possibly affect a man/boy. When it comes to being diagnosed it is just harder to diagnose it in girls.

Remember that I am **NOT** a professional, I just wanted to share some interesting things I have learnt about on my journey since I was diagnosed.

# AM I BEING LAZY OR IS IT MY ADHD?

This is more of a combination of things that I struggle with, some of the things I have found too embarrassing and personal to speak about to others. Since I have started writing about my ADHD, I have become more aware of my own personal traits. Also, I didn't realise just how many people suffer with the same traits as I do, which makes me feel like I'm not alone. This is why I'm telling you about my personal experiences, so you can show or pass on my traits and struggles to help others feel less isolated!

Also, my whole goal for this is to raise awareness. I have noticed a lot of my parents and teachers are wanting to learn and have a better understanding. What better way to learn than to read a personal and honest account from someone who is always going to suffer with it. So, I'm going to tell you everything I can to raise as much awareness as possible.

If you have a child who has ADHD and is struggling with these traits, then, tell them that they have to **ACCEPT** themselves and learn to adapt their daily life around themselves! We will all, eventually get where we want to be, but it will take time. **YOU** will get there.

I get asked questions like:

'How will you overcome that?'
'Tell me how you will fix that problem?'
'How have you got yourself through the bad times?'

Well, the answer is …

**I HAVE ABSOLUTELY NO IDEA**. I still struggle **MASSIVELY** every day with things that I am embarrassed about. I think the most important thing is to accept yourself or those who are struggling with ADHD. We won't **EVER** be able to **FIX** ourselves. **If someone doesn't accept you for who you are, they aren't worthy of your time.** You just personally have to learn to **COPE**.

**YOU DON'T NEED TO CHANGE!**

I have **RECENTLY STARTED TO** accept that I will have days that are going to be harder than others. I just have to learn to take little steps and slow down. Every step I take is one step closer to where I want to be.

I used to think I was **STRANGE** because my daily struggles are other people's **natural** daily routines. It's embarrassing but I find it hard to remember simple things, that everyone is capable of doing:

- Brushing my teeth.
- I find it hard remembering to have a shower.
- Remembering to but deodorant on.
- Remembering to eat and drink enough throughout the day.
- To know when I'm being **"TOO"** much.
- Being **"TOO LOUD."**
- If what I'm doing is inappropriate.
  - Knowing what other's intentions are.
  - Remembering that I have responsibilities.

Remembering to put my clothes out to be washed and then having nothing to wear for weeks because I forgot to do the laundry.

**Things are naturally harder to cope with when you have ADHD.**

Obviously, I'm not saying ADHD is worse than anxiety or autism or any of the other different mental health conditions. Anyone who has any type of mental health issue are stronger than they believe. We all have to fight incredibly difficult battles in our own heads **EVERYDAY.** It doesn't ever get any easier to cope with!!!

I think the key to **"FIXING IT"** is accepting that we aren't going to permanently change ourselves. We just have to **TRAIN** our minds, to do the **NORMAL** functions required in daily life.

Trust me you aren't alone. Even if it's just **ME AND YOU**, you still aren't alone ... there's 2 of us ... HAHA.

I wear the same things **PRETTY MUCH EVERYDAY**. I could go days without taking a hoodie off and changing it. Sounds disgusting doesn't it? But I wear hoodies as a comfort thing. It really helps with my anxiety and ADHD traits. Hoodies are the only thing that I feel comfortable in. My mum has to practically peel it off me. When I take one hoodie off another one goes straight on.

I sometimes think about the fact that I can occasionally be "Slack" with my personal hygiene. **YES**, I am cringing writing this, as I feel so vulnerable and embarrassed by it. This is just something that I struggle with,

because in my mind sitting down watching YouTube or cuddling my mum or my dog Woody is **WAYYY** more important than showering or something along those lines.

I just find things very difficult when I'm in charge of my own personal hygiene, I have no motivation. It is especially hard when I have to do things on my own, I get easily distracted and bored and when I end up getting bored, I simply don't bother doing it again, unless I really have to. **My PARENTS REMIND** me I need to have a bath or brush my teeth, but instead, I'll just sit around and waste time.

Time management is not one of my **BEST** qualities.
But I do try. I know that you try too. Just hang in there. Keep going!

If you're the parent or teacher of a child that is personally struggling with this ...
Help them by:

• Gently reminding them.
• Let them know they aren't the only one struggling.
• Encourage them to buy new clothes or toiletries or buy them for them. (if too young to earn money)
• Just let them know you're there for them.

THAT'S THE MOST IMPORTANT THING.

# ONE OF OUR HIDDEN "SUPERPOWERS" IS MASKING

I have personally struggled with feeling as though I'm **NEVER** good enough to be accepted for who I am. So, I change who I am in order to fit in. I know I'm not the only one. So, let me try to explain what goes on when our ADHD or even AUTISM allows us to **MASK** who we are.

**BUT** before getting into the subject of masking too deeply, I want to give you an explanation of my experience with "Masking."

**How and when I do it and what masking actually is.**

I don't expect everyone to understand the concept of Masking fully.

ADHD can make you feel like you're living a lie. I know I personally do. We are able to create many different versions of ourselves in order to fit in to whichever environment we are currently in. We are usually able to do it in order to hide our ADHD traits. We are well aware that we are overpowering and in your face. All our differences have been pointed out to us **SO** many times before.

Most people say our traits are:

- Irritating.
- Unnecessary.
- Annoying.
- Strange.
- Obnoxious.
- Immature.

Because we are so aware of how people can feel around us. We try our hardest to filter them out so we can fit in with the particular group of people we are with. So, if I'm aware they don't like me being **LOUD**, I'll be vigilant about the volume of my voice, or if I'm aware others don't like me being too **HYPER,** I will try to keep all my hyperactive side of me as calm as possible for as long as possible.

This frequently happens to me and to **A LOT** of others with ADHD too. Personally, I have lost count of how many different identities I actually have actually created. Along with the lies and stories I've made up in order to make my character more believable. I spend most days worrying that someone will expose my many identities and I will look like a compulsive liar. I have had this happen many times before. I have had to pretend I'm into things like:

- Drinking loads of alcohol.
- Going out clubbing.
- Or that I Have **LOADS** of friends.
- I also make up things like having plans with my "boyfriend" or one of my many "friends."

And believe me when I say **LOADS MORE**.

Honestly, I Don't know why, but I'm like a chameleon. I have to hide who I really am because to me that is the only way I am **EVER** meant to fit in. I'm just not a likeable person. It's as if I have a contagious disease; everyone seems to avoid me like the plague.

 There is only about 3 people in this crazy world who actually know the true Molly. They are my parents and my younger sister. No one else knows me. I'm too scared to let people into my life. I'm not going to lie; I am ashamed of myself for lying about who I am. The thing is though, it's like I have this superpower that's got the ability to camouflage my ADHD. It has become so natural like turning on a switch. I prefer to just make up another version of myself rather than trying to explain what ADHD is. I'm fed up with having to try and fit in. I shouldn't feel like I need to change in order to make friends, but I do.

**NOBODY DESERVES TO FEEL ASHAMED OF WHO THEY ARE BECAUSE OF THEIR DISABILITY**.

I finally managed to get myself a best friend. It lasted **A LOT** longer than I was anticipating. It lasted a good, few years. I met her when I had just left school, it was **HONESTLY** the best time of my life. I **HAD** never had a friend like her; her family were like my own. But as we started to hang out more, I started to do the "Camouflage masking thing." Because we were both getting older, it was becoming more apparent to me just how "different" I actually was.

She would have house parties and I would feel like **I HAD** to go, or she wouldn't be my friend. So, I used to go and make my parents ring me up after an hour or so and say that I needed to get home as there was a family emergency; there wasn't but I just couldn't handle it. She began dating boys and started getting serious with her boyfriend. That was when I started to become selfish; I felt so angry and jealous. She had started to be with him more than me. I selfishly started to feel like I just wanted them to break up. That way I could have my best friend's full attention back. I was missing having a best friend or even just a friend in general. It broke my heart, **(you would have thought by now I would have been used to it)**.

After a few months she had started to hit "milestones" that I had **NOT** yet. Because I felt so "behind" (for my age. I ended up making up stories that I had slept with a boy just to avoid the questions about my sex life. I felt that, if I didn't tell her that I hadn't had sex she wouldn't find me weird and would still want to be my friend, as I was hitting the same "milestones" she was. In the end I believe this was what had ended our friendship.

I was under **so** much pressure from **myself**. I just wanted to fit in. Making up lies in order to keep her as my friend definitely wasn't my brightest idea. It never made anything easier, in fact it just snowballed out of control. In the end I became so angry and jealous. I began to hate her because of my jealousy. I started to believe I was doing the right thing by lying about things to keep her as my friend but in the end, I started to feel like a bad person. I hated lying but now it had become a natural part of my life. Every day I was making up lies to make me look cooler than I was/am.

It is **SOOOOO** scary to look back on now. When I was the younger Molly, even my own **BEST FRIEND** never knew the true Molly. I hate talking about this now as I feel embarrassed and inadequate. But the thing is, I know by talking about these things I can hopefully help someone else in the same position I was in, or even help prevent them from taking the same route I did. If someone doesn't accept you for your **QUIRKS**,  they aren't worthy of your friendship. You are better off alone. If someone doesn't help pick you up when you fall, they won't bring anything helpful to a friendship, it will just end up with you hurting. You are the best version of yourself, no other made-up personality can stand a chance against the real you!!!

### We do it without even realising that we are MASKING our ADHD symptoms.

It's so natural to me that not even my family outside my household can tell when I'm having a hard time with my ADHD. If I was having a panic attack in public **NOBODY WOULD KNOW**. I've learnt to deal with my anxiety in my own head, without letting it take over and ruin my day. But to be honest not even my dad knows the full extent to my anxiety. My mum is the only person who truly knows me and understands my CRAZY MIND!

Those of us with ADHD, socially mask ourselves to fit in with our peers; we do this out of fear of rejection. I may have it worse than others, I'm not saying **EVERYBODY** has does this, but I just wanted to share my personal experiences with those that do, or those parents or teachers that have a child that is suffering from this problem and who does use masking to hide it.

### Recently it got to the point where I honestly thought I had the worst case EVER of THE compulsive liar disorder or something.

I used to keep it to myself because it was so embarrassing to me. I used to fear my parents bumping into someone I knew who I had previously made up a different version of myself to. I would worry just in case they spoke to someone without me being there and ask about one of the things I had lied about, things Like drinking or whatever else I'd made up. I felt so lost a lot of the time due to not being able to be who I am around anyone. I made my own world so much **MORE** isolated. Not even my teachers or my college tutors knew who I really was. I wish I had told someone about this sooner.

But I **FINALLY** braved it and told my mum just after I was diagnosed last year. I felt it was something I **NEEDED** to get off my chest. Now that I had finally got an answer, I told her. She told me that she knew - and had known for years; she'd often had to go along with conversations she'd had no idea about. She also told me that was the reason my sister didn't like going out with me, because she said I always tried to "**big myself up**" in front of people.

It's true. I look back now, and it was so noticeable. Masking was and still is my way of coping in situations: situations that I have absolutely **NO** control over or where I feel someone might judge me. So, I just adapt myself to them and go along with whatever they are saying. Knowing full well I'm nothing like what I'm making myself out to be. I could honestly give an author millions of ideas for characters that I have made up around myself.

But now I want to explain about how it has recently started to get on my nerves. It can be a skill to be able to Mask and adapt to any situation, but it also has the potential to make things a lot worse. It can potentially muck stuff up, **BIG TIME.** It hasn't mucked anything up BIG TIME for me recently but that's because I'm so

experienced at doing it. I don't always know when I'm camouflaging myself, but I have recently had a few people say things to me that just annoyed me. So, I thought I would share my experiences with you guys.

I had to put in a formal grievance to my work company. I'm currently going through hell and back with this issue. But because of this I have been made to move locations to help with my anxiety. I have to admit this has been a lot more beneficial than what I had originally thought it would be. But then you guys know it's hard for us with ADHD to establish professional relationships/friendships at the best of times, let alone when you are forced into a group of people you don't know at all.

Since moving location I have had to explain myself, I have trouble with deciding whether to tell them who I actually am or even whether I should explain to them about my ADHD. Due to being bullied, I feel as if I need to pre-warn people about my ADHD quirks, so I don't look strange, or so they don't think I am just being annoying or making things hard on purpose.

So, I have been having weekly meetings at work with my manager. It's meant to be about how they can help me in the workplace, but we all know that **NEVER** actually **HAPPENS**. Anyway, I had my weekly meeting with my manger, and she was asking the usual questions like; how are you? How are you finding working at that location? Is there anything we can do to help you? For a start I was thinking in my head: well, maybe start with sorting the bullying out and actually treating me as the victim not the person who is doing the bullying.

But thankfully I had taken my medication, so I just sat there and listened to that little voice in my head talking and chuckling about the whole situation. Then she said '...

anything new you wanna talk about, or any medical issues I need to know about.' So, I thought I would bring up the fact that I had been referred for an Autism assessment. I was met with, ' ... you don't have autism. I can tell. You don't look like you have it so I can't see it being autism at all.'

'What do you mean by, looking like I don't have autism?' Her reply '... well you just don't look like you have ADHD OR AUTISM.'

I was getting to the point where I just wanted to walk out but then I started thinking about you guys! I may not look like I have ADHD or autism, but it's **INVISIBLE**. No one knows how much or what I'm actually going through. I could be having one of my **BIG PANIC ATTACKS** and if you didn't know me or came to speak to me at work about something simple like a train time, you wouldn't have the slightest clue.

I've been at work, having a **HUGE** mental panic attack and I have had to hold my tears in. I've had to force myself to not drop to the floor and start frantically rocking back and forth with my hands over my ears, and with my eyes tightly shut, shaking loads and as pale as a ghost. No one knows how much strength it takes to hold all that in and having to act normal and interact with people to hide the fact you just want to scream and breakdown.

It's like I'm wearing a mask when I'm in public, and when I step in my house, I peel it off and all my emotions come pouring out of me like, when you shake a bottle of fizz and then open it right after and it explodes everywhere. That is how I feel every day. Some days are worse than others, but I just have to let it all out when I see my mum and dog, they are the only ones I can truly feel safe around and not like I'm being annoying or a pest. This is why I have written a book, because we need to stop this crazy stigma about **not looking like you have ADHD or autism.**

I have to go to work every day with thousands of worries and thoughts swimming round in my head all before 6am in the morning. I have to force myself to talk to people. I have to physically and mentally prepare myself for those 5 hours of work a day. I have to go on my mobile phone millions of times to just check the time, because I just need to be in my comfort zone. It might sound silly but honestly without my phone I don't know how I would survive those few hours at work away from my mum and my dog Woody.

I text my mum within the first 20 mins of work, with a worry I have that is absorbing all my mental capacity. I have to be reassured that nothing bad is going to happen to me. I know that no one can guarantee that, but just having that text from my mum saying there's nothing wrong with me and I'll be fine, gets me through the next hour until I need her to say it again. I may be 21 but I don't know how I will ever move out or even trust anyone even just a little bit.

These situations happen regularly for me. Whenever I open up to someone I'm knocked back with, 'oh, I wouldn't have thought you had that' ... well, **thank you for the sympathy**. It's so patronising towards those of us that suffer with it. Thankfully, I don't have any physical problems or symptoms. I'm very thankful for that, but sometimes it makes you feel as though your condition isn't important. As though it is in some way less important than one that you can physically see. I just wish someone would care or try to understand what we have to fight in our heads every day. It's not easy. Now that I have a diagnosis, I feel like it's being used as an excuse to treat me like I'm crazy and making it all up. I feel so sorry for those that don't have a supportive family like mine. I couldn't do it without mine, especially my mum. I wouldn't be here without you mum! You are one of a kind. I can't thank you enough for being my best friend and my rock when I needed you the most.

If you are reading this and you struggle with this don't be afraid to tell someone your struggling with being socially accepted. It's better to get it off your chest. You don't realise how heavy it is until you tell someone, and the weight magically disappears. It's so much easier to breathe once you've told someone who you are, either with **ADHD OR ANY MENTAL HEALTH STIGMA!**

# WHAT IS NORMAL?

Something that crosses my mind on a daily basis is the question I ask myself.

## WHY can't I just be NORMAL?

I find myself thinking about this **A LOT**. I just want to do all the things, that other people my age are doing. For some reason, it's the life I really **DESIRE** so very badly. I don't think I really understand how my ADHD works. I start to think about all the things I've missed out on, and then I can get myself into a really dark mental or emotional HOLE that I just can't seem to to drag myself out of once I get myself into it. I seriously cannot control my emotions and frustrations. These are some of the hardest things I have to deal with daily. This is when things become extremely overwhelming, and I start letting my anxiety and ADHD run away with my thoughts; then it completely takes over my mindset. It can be a very dark and isolating place, when you allow your emotions to overtake your thoughts, honestly, it is really hard to win back the control to overcome your impulsive thoughts. It's like trying to take the iPad off your kids; it's pretty much impossible.

All us people, that suffer from ADHD or similar conditions want, is to be understood and appreciated. We don't ever get accepted for who we are. We just get mistaken for a troublemaker or as anti-social.

We communicate differently to others; we don't have the same thought processes. We would rather just think about the consequences after. We can't help that; we have a chemical imbalance, and it makes things a lot harder for us to control and our impulsive behaviour can create tension with others. One thing for definite, is the effects of our ADHD traits can make **FITTING IN A LOT HARDER**, as many people don't have the patience, for our sometimes-testing behaviours. I would love to be able to naturally make some friends. I just want one friend **is that SOOOOOOO MUCH TO ASK? I have a lot to offer a friendship. Well, my mum says I do. I think she's pretty biased HAHA.**

I used to believe I wasn't normal because I don't drink alcohol and I don't do drugs. I **PRIDE** myself upon not giving into the peer pressure I was sometimes put under, being a teenage girl at school and college. I'm **PROUD** that I have the self-respect to not allow myself to fall down those tricky paths. Personally, I don't think I would be able to pull myself out of those tricky situations that come along with alcohol and drugs.

With my ADHD I have the combined type of ADHD; I have an obnoxiously strong trait called:
**IMPULSIVENESS** and **OBSESSIVENESS**.

I know that if I personally allowed myself to get involved with anti-social antics, it would give me the negative **BUZZ** that, for some reason my mind craves so badly. It was the buzz I got when I was at school and would run away from teachers or treat them like rubbish. If I were to get that negative buzz involving more serious authority figures, I don't know what type of trouble I would be capable of getting myself into.

I'm explaining this to you as I have had to **MASK** who I am in order to get that **BUZZ** from other social situations. For example, in work situations I tend to be very loud and talkative. It's not negative attention it's almost like I just crave attention and acknowledgment as nobody really bothers to make conversations with me otherwise.

I have personally had to **MASK**, **LIE** or whatever you want to call it, in order, to get by. I have had to make up stories, that I drink (alcohol) and do drugs to try and fit in. I believed that if lied it would make me look like I'm not the **FREAK** that doesn't leave her bedroom. Then once I reflect on this, I think about how much of an idiot I must have looked. Then for a few days afterwards I can't stop beating myself up over it. But at that time, it was my natural instinct to try and find a way that I might be able to fit in with my peers. I believe it's called fight or flight; a mechanism human's have that allows them to react quickly to life-threatening situations. This helps someone to fight off the threat or to (flight) flee to safety.

The mind can overreact to situations that are not at all life-threatening and I always choose to fight the situation, without thinking of the possible consequences from lying or masking the truth. I'm just scared of people knowing the real me! So, I choose to lie (FIGHT) making up stories in my head, and sometimes I'm so believable, I start believing it myself.

So, this is something I wanted to write about, as I know I can't be the only one out there that has to pretended to be someone they aren't in order to fit in? I suffered in

silence for ages, as I was too embarrassed to openly tell my parents about the lying/masking.

I always think to myself after these conversations happen:

*Do you think they knew I was lying?*
*Do you think they picked up that I changed my story about 50 times?*

So, I've been trying really hard recently not to try so hard to be liked and accepted so much. Thankfully, my ADHD medication gives me that well needed time to think before I speak. Personally, I think I have benefited from medication, which is **GREAT**, as I feel like I'm almost seen as **NORMAL.** (whatever that is). Although sometimes, I still find myself making up stories to make myself feel better, which is annoying but that's OK I'm still working on it. ADHD isn't ever going to just disappear, it's here to stay and I'm now working alongside ADHD instead of working against it. It makes things a lot easier.

ADHD can have its positives as well, once you learn to embrace **IT** you will realise just how amazing and lucky you are to be given this special superpower, we **ALL** call ADHD.

I'm going to tell you about some of the things I find hard when it comes to the issues I have with self-doubt and self-worth; the troubles I have when it comes to being "**NORMAL**."

 I work with the public, so I encounter **MANY** people over my 5-hour shift. I see a variety of people, differing in age, gender, weight, or social group; young people from my age

range and older, but it doesn't matter what age they are, they will more than likely have something that I don't. I'm never good enough, and I always believe my negative thoughts.

**I ask myself these questions very frequently:**

- **WHY AREN'T I LIKE THEM?**
- Why can't I have friends like them?
- Why can't I be pretty like her, then maybe I would have more friends?
- Why can't I just like to drink alcohol and like clubbing, that would make me have more friends?
- Why can't I be skinny then maybe I would have a boyfriend?
- Why don't I have a car like that, maybe people would like me more if I had more money?
- Why don't I have friends, I would be so kind to them?
- Why can't I go on a girl's holiday with a group of friends? Oh yeah Molly, you don't have any friends! That's why Molls.
- Why can't I have a baby? So, I can have that life, that gives you **AMAZING** social media likes and a following.
- Why don't I get likes on my photos or Facebook posts?
- Why am I cursed with a mental health illness?
- Why can't I just move out and have the same amount of independence most people my age have?
- If I started smoking would it make people like me More?
- What if I told people I had a boyfriend would it make them think I'm prettier or have a lot more to offer than what I actually do?

- Why aren't I like those girls, that live their lives to the fullest and enjoy it?
- Why can't I get a boyfriend?
- Why can't I make myself go to music festivals? Why can't I just make myself go clubbing?
- Why can't I just make myself enjoy **NORMAL** things, people my age enjoy doing?

Those are some of the things that I ask myself **DAILY!** When I say daily trust me, there's not a day that goes by where I don't self-doubt myself and compare myself to others. I'm just so sorry for myself because I just don't have what others have.

I feel embarrassed that I don't have any friends.
I feel this **HUGE** pressure to have a boyfriend and it's something that depresses me **A LOT**. I feel that when I go to family functions, they are all judging me and wondering why I don't have a boyfriend. I just ask myself **WHY?!**

**WHY CAN'T I JUST BE NORMAL?**

Why can't I just go away on holiday, have a boyfriend or whatever it is?

Unless you have to deal with this you don't realise how much it affects your daily life. I just want to feel like I fit in somewhere without having to create another version of myself. I just want someone to **LIKE ME - FOR ME!** And accept me for my flaws and all my quirks, but I just don't seem to fit in anywhere.

I'm scared if I tell people who I really am they won't like me. Sometimes I'm ashamed to be

**MOLLY**. Honestly, it's hard to deal with, I just wish I had a lot of talents to make me feel worthy. Sometimes, I just want to be someone else.

If I could create a new version of myself it would be:

- Someone Who likes to party.
- Someone Who likes to go out with friends.
- Someone who enjoys being the leader in a group, but **NATURALLY,** not by becoming overwhelmingly obnoxious because of my ADHD traits.

# How does my ADHD make me feel about Sex and relationships?

I have to try and take the attention off my flaws and hide the fact that I'm struggling **A LOT** socially with anxiety. But most importantly I don't have much knowledge on how to act, according to the rule book of socialising: which I obviously didn't take out of the school library and **READ.** I just don't know how to make friends without needing to change who I am, depending on the type of people I'm around. I wish I was someone who could work lots of hours at work and earn loads of money; someone who enjoys having sleepovers and could actually sleep somewhere other than my mum's bedroom floor.

I would love to be more like my sister, I look up to her, it should be the other way around as I'm the oldest. She is a strong, independent, intelligent young lady who is a "go getter." Once she sets herself a goal, she absolutely **SMASHES IT!** She has loads of people that like her, she reminds me of a lion. In my mind it symbolises, deathless courage, strength, fearlessness, bravery, and royalty. She takes on whatever challenge is thrown her way with very little emotional trauma just the pure determination to better herself and prove others wrong. She portrays herself as royalty and so she should. She is a natural leader, has expensive taste in clothes and has an eye for fashion. When I grow up, I want to be just like MY SISTER!

Sometimes I forget just how good I have it. But there's other times when I just wish I wasn't born with ADHD. I think of it more as a curse but since writing a blog to help others, I have started to appreciate my own differences. I wonder if it'll ever get any easier. Will I ever accept the fact that I'm not like others? When will I allow myself to move forward and explore the crazy world of ADHD?

I can't try preaching positivity without really telling you the truth. It is hard and it does come with many **MANY** challenges. However, once you learn to believe in yourself; and I do know just how difficult it is to be able to change and control your emotions and mindsets (much easier said than done), but if you try taking small steps, one day at a time you will appreciate your journey **A LOT** more. You will be able to look back and see the difficulties you have overcome, and most importantly just how much you have achieved mentally and physically. You will get there eventually and once you do you will honestly have so much more self-respect, and self-belief along with a huge sense of fulfilment. Then, you will go on to keep achieving even greater things!

Keep being **YOU**. Be **HAPPY**. Be the **BEST** version of **YOURSELF!**

There is only one of you and you are the Best! I'm going to let you know how ADHD affects my personal life, specifically my self-esteem, confidence, and personal relationships. This isn't going to be a guide about how to get boyfriends, or what I like in personal relationships, it's going to be about how I feel **ABOUT** relationships. I asked people to tell me what they wanted to know about my experiences and this one popped up a lot. So, I thought that I would try and put my feelings into words about this particular subject as it's something that I find very hard.

So, I know that I'm not alone in this, but I haven't ever been in a long-term relationship. I have only had boyfriends here and there but nothing that has amounted to anything more than school kid puppy love. I worry so much about my appearance, weight, and skin **A LOT**.

I think even without having ADHD a lot of young girls and boys will feel the same way I do. The pressure from social media makes us feel that we have to look like the Instagram models to be classed as "beautiful." It creates a lot of problems with self-esteem and relationships. But having ADHD makes things a little harder for us. We fixate on things to the point of obsession. So, when it comes to picking out my own insecurities I have absolutely no problem calling myself:

- Fat.
- Ugly.
- Too curvy.
- Spotty.
- Too broad shouldered.

Or pointing out that my teeth aren't straight or white enough. I pick myself apart about my **FLAWS**, then I compare myself to the girls I see as "perfect." The ones who have flat stomachs, toned abs, or clear skin.

Yes, I know you don't have to have ADHD to feel like this, yes, I know that most teenagers all go through these stages. But What people don't realise, is having  ADHD makes things seem like the end of the world. We fixate on things and become overly sensitive and obsessed. When in reality the thing we are worried about is something small and unnecessary.

It's like being on a merry-go around and it not stopping to let you off. It just goes around and around until you jump off; metaphorically speaking, you get angry and frustrated with yourself and in my case, you take it out on others.

It can be very lonely and isolating when you get fixated on your flaws as you begin to believe that everyone else sees you the way you see yourself. This is something that continually affects me, I don't have any secret tricks to get over this particular issue. But what I can honestly say, is my mum once said something to me, that always helps me through this issue:

'If someone doesn't love you for who **YOU** are **THEN THEY AREN'T WORTH YOUR TIME AND THEY DON'T DESERVE YOUR KINDNESS.**'

This paragraph is a sensitive issue for me right now, but I like being honest and open with you guys. As I want this to potentially help someone else to be able to approach their child, or a student which may be struggling with this situation. There will always be others going through this alone, and if I can reach out with this, then it might just help them get the help and support they need and deserve.

So, I have developed a bad eating disorder. I'm not going to label it as anorexia, as I haven't had a formal diagnosis yet, but it has got to the point where the number on the scale determines how:

- Much I allow myself to eat.
- My moods are afffected.
- Much effort I make that day to look nice.

- Much I enjoy my day.
- I feel towards others.

I get very, **VERY,** angry, and depressed if I put weight on. It's an obsession. I am obsessed with my weight and yes, this is a part of my ADHD. It's how my impulsive behaviour comes out. I can't control my impulsive emotions, and thoughts over this situation, I can't just simply "stop." It's not as easy as that. Believe me I've tried and sometimes you have to ask for help.

**IT IS NOT** ok to punish yourself over the number on the scales ... **YOU ARE WORTH MORE THAN ANY NUMBER ON THE SCALE ... YOU ARE BEAUTIFUL.**

My ADHD as I've got older has become more self-destructive. I allow myself to be horrible about myself and have let myself fall into bad mindsets and habits.

This is how it affects women. (obviously, it can happen to men also) Women are more likely to end up with an eating disorder when they have ADHD. It's our body's way of releasing the impulsiveness and compulsiveness.

In absolutely **NO** way am I saying **THAT** men don't suffer from this, but it's **SCIENTIFICALLY** Proven that women are 3 times more likely to be affected then men are with ADHD.

**SOOOO**, here we are talking about personal

relationships, something I find very difficult to understand. I get very attached to people. I'm not diagnosed with any attachment disorders, but I certainly do have an issue with it. I am a very vulnerable person; I can't

tell what other people's intentions are. Even, if you were to be the nastiest person around, I'd still think that you would be nice to me. I don't see the bad things about someone until something happens to me, and even then, I blame myself.

I usually blame my ADHD but I'm being assessed for Autism at the moment, and the likelihood I have it is extremely high. I have no understanding of other's emotions or relationships. They are like a foreign language to me.

So, how I deal with relationships may be different to you, but I honestly think there's something else going on in my crazy head, so don't worry if you don't get what I'm going on about. (I normally don't know what I'm going on about either.)

So, when it comes to boys, I can't seem to get to grips on how I should act; what is appropriate or what is inappropriate.

- I always feel like I can't say no.
- I feel like I have to be skinny for a guy to like me.
- I set a lot of boundaries around myself making it hard to deal with inside my head.

It's as if I'm trying to find a word, in a word search that isn't even in the word search. So, you end up wasting your time searching for the answer when you really didn't need to. I end up allowing myself to get involved in situations that could become dangerous.

I don't ever see what the other persons intentions are towards me. I get so attached to the idea of having a friend I will do anything to keep them happy and to keep them being my friend.

Whereas to everyone else they are obvious, in my mind it's just a list of their personality traits, but to others it's like they can see the hidden dangers almost instantly. It's as if they are invisible to me, which is scary sometimes.

I sit back and think about stuff, then it clicks that I could have gotten myself in a very dangerous situation and I end up scaring myself. I end up having a panic attack about the "what ifs," but it doesn't stop me the next time. It's like a continuous struggle I have. I'm very vulnerable when it comes to people.

When a guy shows the slight bit of interest in me, my mind automatically starts working overtime, I start thinking about:

- What our kids would look like.
- Meeting his parents.
- Moving in together.
- Going on holidays.

Basically, I plan my whole life with this person after he says, 'You're beautiful' or even just 'HI' It's as if my mind is just not capable of having any type of safeguarding or concern for my own safety.

I used to accept random boys on Facebook, if they spoke to me, I used to literally talk to strangers. I have absolutely no concept of stranger danger. It's so scary to talk about it because it makes me realise how much danger I have exposed myself to in the past.

I want to write about this in my book, as it's a part of my journey and I want to be open and honest because that's the whole reason for my book; to help others understand.

So here it goes, sex isn't something I'm interested in at all. The thought of it makes me feel physically sick. The idea of having to be alone with someone in a situation where you are at your most vulnerable is something that makes me extremely uncomfortable.

I won't allow myself to be in that situation. Yes, this is an issue. Yes, it's probably something that is going to affect future relationships. Yes, I'm guessing it's going to be something that is going to affect me for my entire life. I spoke about this to my specialist and I was delighted to know that is isn't just me, it is a trait of autism. So, now I know that it's something that I may never be completely ok with. And it's been something that I've kept a secret in my heart for a long time. I've never spoken to anyone about how I truly feel, as I thought that I had to be having sex to be normal.

I've made so many lies up to people saying that I have slept with people to just make me feel normal. However, once I spoke openly about my worries and concerns to my mum, she helped me come to terms with all of this.

I've had to learn that things I believe I should be doing **OR** which I see my younger sister doing isn't always going to happen the same way for me, or anyone else with ADHD. We just aren't allowing ourselves to flourish in our own time. I may only be speaking for myself here. Not everyone is going to be repulsed by intimate relationships or friendships but I am. Please, don't judge me for this. It's very sensitive and has taken a lot of courage to write about this in my book, as it's putting me in a very vulnerable position.

I don't think I'll ever be in a relationship and that is ok. I haven't always thought like this trust me. It has **NOT BEEN** easy to get to this point. I think in today's society we are made to believe we are inadequate if we aren't in a relationship. It's very, **VERY** difficult for me as a person to be in a relationship. I am seeking help for this. I don't know what my issue is, I don't know why but it isn't easy for me, not easy at all.

I put so much pressure on myself to try and find a boyfriend, and I feel as if I'm not reaching the milestones, I set myself in my head. I see myself as a failure, like I'm disappointing my family by not having a boyfriend. I hate going to family functions because I dread the question '... got yourself a young man Molly?' What do I say to that? Nobody understands how much of a mental **STRUGGLE** it is for me to get a boyfriend. It isn't as easy, for those of us with ADHD.

It's either we are giving our all or nothing at all. It adds so much pressure. I end up taking it out on myself. I get so worked up trying to convince myself that I'm going to go on a date and be OK. But just the thought is enough to start a meltdown. For others it will be a lot more natural and that's OK. I'm so happy that this doesn't affect a lot of ADHD suffers, and I also think this is a mixture of ADHD and more than likely autism, so please don't worry if you don't understand this

100%. It's not always going to be that way for everyone, as not everyone suffers from the same things.

# STiGMA MYTHS AND ACTUAL FACTS ABOUT ADHD

The stigma behind our illness ADHD, has personally affected me. I also know that many of you will more than likely have been affected by this too.

Facts about ADHD:

**ATTENTION DEFICIT HYPERACTIVITY DISORDER**

I have researched these from several books, and I have adapted them into my own description. They are, 100% genuine.

The symptoms of ADHD make it very hard for someone with it to learn both academically and self-discipline. It also affects how they interact with others; socialising with others their own age can become a real issue. This means that the child or teenager are more likely to have come across issues in school/college with friendships, discipline, and academic studies: they can struggle and be left behind, leading to even more issues. The child/teenager might start to misbehave in lessons in order to hide the fact that they are struggling academically. Emotionally it can take its toll on someone who is constantly having to hide the fact that they are struggling and trying their hardest just to fit in.

ADHD is a complex disorder; it is still not fully understood even by some of the medical professionals.

Because of this ADHD is **easily** misunderstood by so many. This has made it hard for those who suffer with the condition to actually get the help they require. For example, women are more likely to go through childhood and even most of their young adulthood without getting a diagnosis. Girls/women have more of an ability to **MASK** their symptoms of ADHD in order to fit in with their peers; females learn quicker to adapt to their social surroundings.

If you try and speak to shallow minded people, they will tell you that ADHD is a made-up illness. They think its **NAUGHTY KID** syndrome! They see us, as those kids who sit at the back of the classroom disrupting everyone. Little do they know how much that "naughty kid," is trying to cope with one hell of a fight, that's going on in their own head.

ADHD people struggle with things that other people find easy: showing up on time, planning a meal, remembering to take out the recycling ... *on the right day.* Our thought patterns seem to be a lot slower than other people's.

Meltdowns don't always start from **BIG THINGS**. It is a mixture of many small things that happen over a period of time. Our emotions build up and then the small things become overwhelming, triggering a huge meltdown in the ADHD brain.

Things like:

- Homework
- Workplace stress
- A word someone said to you that you found offensive or even just didn't want to hear.

- The disappointment of things not going your way or as you had hoped for.

All these different things can easily snowball into a major meltdown. The response hardly ever reflects the seriousness of the problem.

**Some COMMON ADHD myths:**

It's not a real medical condition - ADHD is caused by a chemical imbalance in the brain. It's a proven medical (neurological) disorder and has been for years.

People with ADHD are just dumb or lazy - Studies show that people with ADHD often have above average intelligence and ADHD doesn't make a person lazy, but it does make them disorganised.

People with ADHD never achieve anything - There are a lot of well-known celebrities that suffer from ADHD, who have all achieved amazing things. So, there is nothing stopping anyone else with ADHD from reaching their potential. Just look at, Justin Timberlake, Channing Tatum, Adam Levine for example

Kids with ADHD will outgrow it - Up to 50% of children with ADHD will still have it in adulthood. Most adults with ADHD are undiagnosed though, and only a minority will seek help and get a diagnosis. Everyone with ADHD is hyperactive - People with the inattentive subtype of ADHD are not necessarily hyperactive. Their hyperactivity exists on the inside, so it can be hard for others to see, that they have hyper thoughts where everything is constantly racing through their mind.

ADHD only affects boys - Girls are just as likely to have ADHD, but it does seem that the type of ADHD which affects girls more is the inattentive type, ADD, whereas boys suffer more often with the hyperactive type. The inattentive type is harder to detect. So, they usually get misdiagnosed.

ADHD is caused by bad parenting - The parents of any child with ADHD or any behavioural condition are **ROCKSTARS!** They are amazing parents who have to put up with so much, yet they still love their child unconditionally and still support them through their struggles. **NEVER** underestimate the power of Parents with ADHD/ADD children.

ADHD didn't exist in the past – Yes, it did ADHD has had several names like mental restlessness, minimal brain dysfunction and hyperkinetic disorder. It has always been around it just had a different name.

People with ADHD aren't intelligent or have any drive to better themselves - Absolutely not true. Some of the most intellectual scientists are on the autism spectrum or have ADHD. So, as you can see there are a lot of things people just don't understand about ADHD.

People just don't understand, that waking up in the morning we don't have to have a coffee to give us that caffeine **BUZZ**.

We don't lack emotions; we are literally drowning in them.

We have emotions running through our body at 50mph, we just can't get control over all of them; that's why sometimes things get a little too much for us. Our, emotions are extremely intense. We feel everything, so we may come across over-sensitive, when really, we just need people to support and help us understand that we are just as good as anyone else. We may have our differences but trust me when I say we are just as important. In fact, we have so much going on in our minds, and as much as we just want it to stop, it doesn't. So, we just have to get through it and that takes a lot of courage.

We can do anything we set our minds on ... don't believe me? Well wait and see what you/your sibling/child will achieve once they have someone who believes in them. They will conquer the world; they just need **YOU** by their side and they will shine.

Work is a **HUGE** struggle for me. I'm currently having a really hard time. I've been told I am being too **SENSITIVE** because of my ADHD. My bosses have suggested that I was lying about being bullied, which has made everything **SOOO** hard for me. I've told them about my struggles, but it just seems to get turned around and used against me.

But underestimating me was their worst mistake. They have thrown everything they can at me and **YES**, there has been a few times recently when I just wanted to give up. However, I have my supporters who are always right beside me. They don't know what they have done, messing with an ADHDer. I come with the power to hyper focus and I have found out so much that I now have enough ammunition to fight them with. My family haven't let me give up or give in to my works attempts to make me feel like I'm in the wrong. What I'm trying to get at, is when we come up against these barriers in our life we have to physically and mentally fight against the anxiety and depression, and quite often the symptoms and traits of our ADHD. They become so much worse when we are stressed. We take it out on those who care for and love us, because we know they won't give up on us. Sometimes, we just need to know that we have people on our team instead of those who always seem to be against us.

Everywhere we go we have to deal with these stigmas and myths about our mental health condition. It gets belittled and pushed aside, considered as being 'a minimal' condition but honestly you, or your sibling, or child with ADHD **ARE SUPERHEROES** ... Please never let them feel alone. When we feel alone, we feel like we are carrying the weight of the world on our shoulders, and just by saying, 'I'm here for you' or 'we will sort this together' makes a massive difference. Just having the feeling of friendship or love is something I can't explain. When everyone always seems to be against us, we just want to be understood and loved. We aren't asking for world peace; we just want to be seen as **NORMAL**.

Having ADHD **DOESN'T DEFINE US!!** The only thing that defines us is the stigma we get, and we can't change that. That's why we need to keep raising awareness. Big companies need to make more of an effort to understand their customers, and even their own colleagues with ADHD. **SCHOOLS AND TEACHERS** need to understand the complexities that come along with ADHD. We aren't given an equal chance. We are seen to just be lazy and annoying, but like I said, give us a chance and you won't regret it!

ADHD is a huge struggle but that doesn't mean we can't achieve great things!

# If you want to help us, Then take our ADHD seriously

I'm stupid for thinking everyone understands me. I'm so vulnerable and naive that I believe everyone has the best intentions at heart. I'm silly for forgetting that I'm not everyone's cup of tea. I get most upset, that I repeatedly let others take full advantage of my niceness and my vulnerability. It's so hard for me to keep letting others into my life as every time I do, I try to do whatever it takes to just keep them as a friend. I lose so much respect for myself because I allow others to treat me like s▮▮▮▮ I haven't ever had a friend that has known the real Molly. It's so sad I'm 21 years old and I have absolutely no friends to talk to or support me through the tough times.

I've been thinking a lot about how I've been feeling and how others make me feel as a person.

The only way I can describe how my life has felt for the past 21 years. It is as if, I'm living inside of a **"HANNAH MONTANA"** TV programme. I'm living 2 separate lives, except neither one makes me happy. When I go out in public, I have to hide my true identity as I know others don't like or can't cope with the true **ME**. I have to change to come across as **NORMAL,** in order to be accepted in society. I feel like I have to lie about who I am and what I've done in my life just to fit in. I change my whole identity, the

 only thing I keep the same is my name; that's how sad it is. I don't know how to be myself around others anymore. I have so many different versions of who I am that I've lost count.

I lost my **BEST FRIEND** at the beginning of this year because I couldn't keep up with the whirlwind of lies, I told her just to hide who I really am. She was the best friend I have ever had. We didn't speak for years and then she got in contact with me last year and I can't even begin to explain how happy I was. Then the reality hit me, that I would have to keep up the lies I told her years ago. So, I started up our friendship **AGAIN** on a bed of complete lies. I decided after a few months that I couldn't cope with the guilt. I wanted to tell her how much I was struggling but if I did, I would have to admit I had lied about everything which would contradict everything, I'd ever told her. I couldn't look that stupid, so I did what I'm best at, ran away from my responsibilities and stopped talking to her completely. It broke my heart. I still think about our friendship every day; we had the best friendship. We could insult each other and be on FaceTime for hours just chatting pure rubbish, which was OK because we were both laughing the whole time. And then, I ruined it, well I didn't my ADHD did. At the minute, I am struggling quite badly, although, I'm not going to burden everyone else with my anxiety and ADHD. However, I wanted to write this to get my feelings down as I know others will be going through this, or perhaps their children will be.

**FRIENDSHIPS ARE HARD FOR ME**! It's my biggest dream to have a proper friendship. I just want her back as my best-friend, but I can't because she doesn't know **MOLLY**, she knows my alter egos the various **MOLLYs** I wish I could be.

This book isn't meant to be negative, but this bit is. I want to help you understand how difficult it can be, and some of the reality of having ADHD. It's not all about challenging behaviour, aggressive children or out of control teenagers. We aren't **BAD** people. We just want to be accepted.

**EVERYWHERE** we go we feel as though we have to change who we are not only to be accepted, but to be able to thrive in the environment. In some situations, we just adapt so as not to be the odd one out and look like an outsider. Our condition, **MAY HAVE ATTENTION** in the name, but we are not always doing things for the attention. It isn't that simple. It's so complex, I wish it was that simple.

**ATTENTION** has so many different aspects to it that I couldn't even begin to explain it. But the attention we get doesn't have to be either good or bad, it's mostly to take the attention away from our insecurities and make us feel like we aren't struggling. It's a coping mechanism that we use to hide the fact that we are vulnerable and usually struggling with anxiety or an emotional meltdown. Sadly though, others look at us like we are just wanting to be the centre of attention or that we are spoilt, and just don't like being told **NO**. It's these sorts of things that ruin our chances of thriving, making us believe that we have to change who we are to fit in and therefore not be alone.
**At school we have to change our behaviour.**
**In society we have to change our behaviour.**

At home we are accepted and that's why we are usually at our worst behaviour or most emotionally

 challenging. At home, we can finally take our mask off and let our all the emotions and frustrations out that we have had to keep

hidden inside, and away from others all day. So, home is our safe place, where we tend to take everything out on our loved ones because we trust you. We know you are there to support us, and we know that you aren't going to judge us ... We love you ...

If only more people could see the other side of us, they would realise that ADHD is our best personality trait; it makes us who we are. We are extra hyper, loud, emotionally sensitive, and behaviourally challenging, but we have such **BIG** hearts which we wear on our sleeves. We are loyal, loving and caring and there is so much more to us than just ADHD. We also have the good side of ADHD ... we are committed, we are in touch with our emotions, we have creative ideas and are always up for a good laugh. We just don't get a chance to show that, because we naturally mask ourselves for fear of being judged and leaving ourselves open to heartbreak; we have experienced those enough times.

If you could see the good side of our ADHD,
underneath it all you would see we are just like you. We don't want to be treated differently, we just want to be accepted and motivated to achieve our goals! And have the freedom to show you who we really are!

Here's a few things that could make relationships and friendships easier if you are trying to help and understand an ADHDer:

- Believe That ADHD Is Real.
- Allow Us Time to Process.
- Don't Dismiss Our Anxiety.
- Understand and accept That We Feel Bad.
- Allow us to express ourselves freely.

- Treat us normally. Don't judge us on our mistakes, we are trying.
- We may need a little more reassurance than most people.
- Know that we aren't perfect, but we are delighted that you are giving us a chance.

Most importantly give us space and support. It's the little things that make the big things easier to control and help us to clear our minds. Don't belittle us, don't make comments like:

'Have you taken your pills?'
'Is that your ADHD?'

These comments can make a good day turn into the worst day in seconds.

Don't be demanding we don't like being told what to do. Change the way you ask us to do something, make it more like a game - don't put us under pressure. Say, can you at some point make the bed, instead of saying can you make the bed now; it makes us feel like we are in control of the situation.

I want you to know that you aren't alone, if you are going through this, it's hard but you aren't alone you have me.

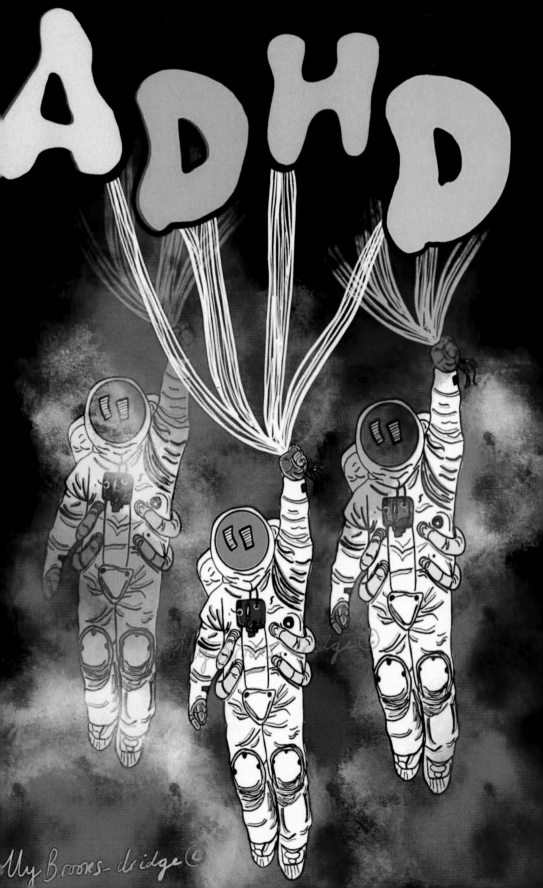

# WHAT WOULD I HAVE TOLD THE YOUNGER MOLLY

This is going to be some of the hardest things you will have to go through, **BUT** I got through them and I know you can too. I have some tips here that will help you survive school, college, and a few other adolescent problems.

My tips are based on my personal experiences and the difficulties I have faced. I'm going to tell you some of the survival tips that I would have appreciated and would love to have heard from someone older than me with ADHD, like a role model or mentor with ADHD.

When I was growing up there wasn't much awareness of ADHD, especially in girls. I never came across anybody who was willing to speak openly to me about either ADHD or anxiety. I was diagnosed in September 2019. So, I went through my childhood and teenage years without understanding any of what made me so different to the other kids. I was told many times flippantly, by teachers as well as the other kids, "you have ADHD, don't you?" Although, I never got tested, so I never received any help or support; I just received detentions and exclusions.

I'm 21 years old and honestly, I am so lost in life. I feel almost like my life is being wasted, while I sit down and

try to figure out what I want to achieve career wise. I seem to spend ages sat wondering what is wrong with my head. The simple answer is I never had anyone to help or encourage me. So, I want to share some simple words of experience and encouragement, to either younger people with ADHD, or even people older or my age, that are in the same boat.

So here goes:

**It's okay to make mistakes** - **EVERYONE** has bad days, and just because they don't have ADHD, it doesn't mean that they can't or won't make mistakes or that they are any better than you. Having ADHD just means we don't learn as quickly, or until we get a little older that we might need some support or guidance to help us make the right decisions. We may take a little longer to learn from our mistakes, but once we do, we honestly thrive. Give yourself time, it's important to let yourself make mistakes, you will eventually get where you want to be. Making mistakes is very normal, it actually helps you become a very successful person.

## IN ORDER TO SUCCEED SOMETIMES YOU HAVE TO FAIL!

Believe me, when I say having ADHD doesn't mean you have failed because you haven't, you have an extra special personality trait that **SOOO** many people are going to **LOVE ABOUT YOU!** It just gives you a few extra ingredients and you're going to make a fantastic a person when you believe you're worthy of success and respect.

**It's okay to have BAD days** - Having a bad day or having a bad week, doesn't mean you have failed either, it just means you need to give yourself a rest. You are trying so hard that your mind just needs a break. ADHD is like your mind running millions of miles a day, it just doesn't stop, and everyone needs a break once in a while. So, please give yourself time to rest. It's so important to care about your incredible mental health; you have to keep it strong in order to **RULE THE WORLD,** which I know that anyone with ADHD is more than capable of achieving!

**It's okay not to be "PERFECT" - NO-ONE** is perfect. Ok maybe **DOGS** are but apart from dogs no one is perfect. Having mental health issues doesn't mean you are worthless or worth anything less than someone who doesn't suffer from depression, anxiety, or ADHD. You need to remember that you aren't defined by your own mental health issues or anything that you can't personally change or control about yourself. **IT'S OK TO NOT BE PERFECT.** It's ok not to have the perfect figure likethe models on social media. You are unique, and there isn't anyone else that can rock being you better than YOU! It's ok to not have the clearest skin, not everyone has crystal clear skin and that doesn't matter. If people don't like you for you then they aren't worthy of your friendship. **YOU ARE PERFECT** and that's all that matters. If you believe in yourself, you can overcome personal barriers. When you believe that you are one of a kind, you will see just how beautiful you truly are! If you are a boy, yes you can be beautiful too! (But I'll say handsome if you prefer.) **It's OK to be true to YOURSELF** - Trust me when I say people would prefer you to be who you truly are as opposed to someone who is fake and lies about themselves, their life or their achievements. Lying won't ever find you the people that truly deserve your company or friendship. If you're honest you will find people will love you for who you are; you need to give yourself a chance and be your awesome self out there in this **CRAZY** world.

**Having no Friends isn't the end of the world** - I've never been the popular girl or the pretty girl. I have always been the loner in the back of the room, shouting and being **SOOO** loud to try and cover up my crippling anxiety.

**I always used to ask myself** - If I had friends would It make me any happier in life? Is It because I have ADHD that no one likes me? Why can't I just be normal?

Well, I'm 21 and I have 0 friends, but I have family and that is something money can't buy; even friendship can't beat that! Well, not for me anyway. I know everyone has different family and friend situations but remember everyone is different. What I'm trying to say, is that while having ADHD does make things a lot harder for us, if someone doesn't like you because you have ADHD, they certainly aren't worthy of your time, because you have one hell of an amazing personality. ADHD gives you so many things that are amazing and that people will love you for.

For example, I am always the one to make people laugh from the pit of their stomachs. I always know how to cheer someone up with my hyper crazy ADHD personality. I always feel other's emotions deeply, which means I will always be there for them. Once you give me your friendship, I value it so much that it might look clingy, but it's only because I so want you to be happy and to keep you as my friend for life. I know I sometimes overdo it, but I don't mean to, I just treasure any friend I have as I don't get or have one very often. But doesn't it just show that we have so many amazing traits.

**It's OK to struggle academically** - The thing that isn't OK is not trying. If you try your absolute hardest you can't fail. Once you try hard you get that sense of self-worth and achievement. It doesn't matter what grades you get as long as you try your hardest, that is what matters. My mum always used to say that to me. Despite being uncontrollable at school I still managed to leave with a decent set of grades. They were not enough to get me into the college course I had always dreamed of, but it was enough to get me through. I'm proud that I got through school, because despite all the obstacles that we ADHD sufferers get thrown at us, we all still manage to achieve great things, regardless of grades or qualifications. I believe if you have self-respect and respect for others, you're already a winner. Love yourself and those around you, because not much else will ever compare to the feeling of being loved and desired. Keep making others smile and feel loved, and in return you will get a priceless sense of worth and self-pride. Keep being you because it will get you a lot further than money ever will.

**One for the pre-teens** - We are usually misunderstood by others our age, because we might not "reach the same milestones" as they do at the exact same time. We may always be a little behind, and that's OK. We are always taught to be in control and be able to juggle multitasking and relationships but trust me it's not easy with ADHD. Sex and peer pressure really kick in around 13/14 years old, and it can make you feel dumb, ugly, and worthless, just remember you aren't. It's just who you are. Your brain doesn't function the  same as everyone else's. Just talk to your parents and teachers if you are struggling, it's OK to ask for help. Don't ever feel embarrassed. There comes a time when everybody needs a little extra support.

It feels much less of a problem when you seek advice. NEVER give in to peer pressure, you are worth much more than that. Be strong and be true to who you are. Like I've said previously, I know it's not always as easy as that, it is much harder than me just preaching it. But once you get through the hard times, you'll look back and see the mountains you've overcome. Trust me, it's an amazing journey learning to love yourself. Don't let ADHD define you because you can use it to your advantage. We do struggle with a lot of things, but you have to remember that you have a gift and that is being strong minded, which may seem overpowering at times, but we can and WILL get through it! Don't give up on yourself and believe in yourself a lot more. **YOU ARE CAPABLE OF ACHIEVING FAR MORE THAN YOU THINK.**

Being normal is boring compared to our crazy ADHD lives. I want you to know that you are going to be fine. Whatever you are going through right now, is simply teaching you a lesson for your future. You need to take notice of the lessons you are being taught because trust me they are valuable. I'm absolutely sure you are going to smash anything you put your mind to. **WE HAVE ADHD AND THAT IS OUR SECRET SUPERPOWER.**

You can achieve anything you put your mind to. ADHD doesn't have to define you. You can use it to your advantage. You have things others don't. You wouldn't believe the benefits ADHD has for us, for example.

- Who else has unlimited amount of energy like we do?
- Who else can think outside of the box like we do?

- Who can make a group of people laugh with our natural humour; without needing to change who we are?
- Who else can hyper focus on homework and get something done in an hour that should have taken you a month?

**NO-ONE** can ... JUST US ... WE ARE LUCKY ENOUGH TO HAVE ADHD.

You can achieve things others might not achieve in a quicker period of time because you have the ability to hyper focus on small details

You should be proud of your ADHD. We can't do anything about the fact that we have it so why not embrace our uniqueness! But remember guys ...
You might be going through a hard time right now but trust me it gets better. The best thing you can do right now is talk to someone. That is the biggest thing I regret. I had a lot of opportunities to speak to someone, but I never did. I was lost and alone. If only I would have just opened-up to someone and told them openly about how much I was struggling, how lost I was then maybe I could have got the help I needed a lot earlier.

**Please guys and gals** ...
Do your future self a favour and talk to someone now; don't leave it too late. You need to help yourself. No one else is ever going to have your best interests at heart like you do. Stick up for yourself and your future. You got this!

 You might be thinking that you aren't normal or that you don't fit in anywhere. **REMEMBER** that those people who don't treat you **NICELY,** or fairly, aren't worth it.

They aren't worthy of your friendship. They don't deserve to have **YOU** in their life. You deserve to be treated like royalty. You have a heart of gold. You only want the best for others. You wouldn't dream of hurting anyone else's feelings like others do yours. Remember don't ever try to change who you are because **WHO YOU ARE IS ENOUGH.** You are an absolutely amazing individual that can take on the world with your ADHD superpower! You just have to learn to love yourself and embrace your differences. **If you are self-conscious remember that you are perfect the way you are.** The most beautiful or attractive thing about a person is self-confidence. You don't need to become selfish or cocky, but you deserve to love yourself, you are perfect. If someone doesn't love you or like you for who you are then they don't deserve you. It's as simple as that guys! If you are going through bullying then you need to remember that the bullies are usually jealous of you, and you have so much for others to be jealous of, for example:

• People with ADHD are very bright, creative, and funny.
• We have the ability to remind the world that perfection is boring and having our own quirks make us special.
• We are like a triple chocolate cookie in a world full of plain chocolate chip cookies ...

**Our extra ingredients make us a lot more appealing. We have great assets to offer anyone.**

We have all faced our share of tough times, but we have managed to adapt our symptoms to fit in to our environments. We have had to learn how to act socially

acceptable and **MANY** other things along our **CRAZY** personal journey with ADHD. All our ADHD
symptoms make us the person we are today, and you are a totally amazing person to be around. We can put smiles on others faces without even trying. We are very determined and motivated people, and when we put our brain to work, we can accomplish incredible things. Honestly take it from me guys. You might think that things are bad now but, in a few days or weeks from now you'll be able to look back and think about how far you have come since then and be proud of your journey; every step is a step closer to being the best version of yourself. **Other people's opinions don't matter**. The most important opinion is the one you have of yourself. Once you start loving yourself and embracing the things you don't like about yourself you will start radiating pure beauty and confidence, and people won't want to mess with that! Hold your up head high and be proud of your differences and your ADHD. It makes you the person you are today and **REMEMBER THAT** person is incredibly **STRONG** and intelligent, and worth every ounce of love and support you get. Don't ever settle for anything less than what you deserve guys! **You can do anything! I believe in you!**

Make yourself some goals and slowly start working towards them. Once you reach your first goals or milestones, you will get this incredibly strong sense of accomplishment. You deserve it because no one but you, understands how complex ADHD is.

**BUT REMEMBER I'M HERE FOR YOU EVERY STEP OF THE WAY!**

# NEVER
# NEVER
# NEVER
# NEVER
# GIVE UP

# Where it all began: when I was born

So, I was born on the 11th of June 1998. Even before I was born, I was causing my parents all kinds of trouble. But mostly my **AMAZING** mum. She was very poorly when she was pregnant with me. She was constantly hospitalised with bad sickness and couldn't move without being sick. For the whole 9 months of her pregnancy, she couldn't eat or drink **ANYTHING** without bringing most of it back up.

My mum was induced at 38 weeks, so I was 2 weeks early, **BUT** during her labour my heartbeat dropped drastically. My mum was told she had to have an emergency **C-SECTION** and I finally made an appearance early on the morning of the 11th of June. I had the umbilical cord wrapped around my neck which was restricting my airways, which was the reason why my heartbeat had dropped. So, you could say I entered the world needing all the attention on me from the very start. **HAHA**.

In all seriousness, I had a traumatic birth, which you could say was nature's way of preparing my parents for the whirlwind that my crazy life was just about to throw at them. That which we now know as ADHD.

Bipolar was a part of my mum's life even before I was born, and sadly after such a stressful pregnancy and traumatic birth experience, she had begun to feel very vulnerable. She became depressed and was officially diagnosed with puerperal psychosis.

When I was only a few days old, my mum was sectioned under the mental health act. I was placed in a psychiatric ward along with my mum. We were both isolated away from my dad and other family members. My mum was only allowed minimal contact with me, and even then, the contact she had with me had to be monitored.

We didn't get to have the special bonding time that a mother and child would usually have. So, it was hard for my mum and myself to have that precious bond, vital for the first few days of the baby's life; that precious nurturing bubble was popped when she wasn't mentally strong enough and needed time to get better herself. Thankfully, my mum wasn't in the psychiatric hospital long, just 1 week. She started to get herself better and was soon ready to be the amazing mum she is today.

All throughout my first year of life I was a very sickly child. I suffered from asthma, very bad colic, and acid reflux. I constantly had a runny nose. I wouldn't lay down on my back at all in the cot which meant that I wouldn't settle properly to sleep in a cot. I had to have constant contact for example, being cuddled or held by either my mum or dad. I would only settle down and sleep in a baby bouncer, the momentum of the bouncing had to be continuous, so my parents would have to sit up all night bouncing the baby bouncer otherwise I would wake up distressed and crying. Also, I wouldn't lay or sit in a pram, I had to be carried around in someone's arms. I would settle in a baby carrier, so even, back then, I was pretty demanding. **HAHA**.

So that was the beginning of my journey, I was told by a professional that there is a strong connection between my birth and my ADHD. Apparently if you were oxygen deprived at birth you have a greater chance

of developing ADHD, which is why I decided to include my birth story. As I believe it could be a strong indication of why I have ADHD. Also, the parents reading this may be able to link a traumatic birth experience with their child's ADHD.

This is my beautiful Mumma bear

**BUT THIS WAS NOT THE END OF MY CRAZY ADHD JOURNEY Keep reading ... It gets more interesting as I get older ... Well, it definitely gets funnier ...**

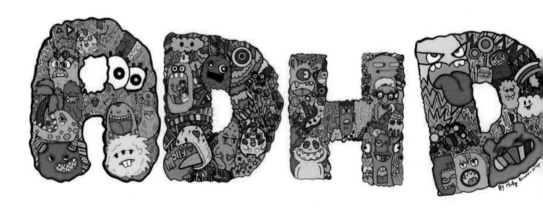

# TODDLERS AND TANTRUMS

Like I said at the beginning I wasn't diagnosed with ADHD until I was 21 years old. So, my childhood was full of misunderstood tantrums, meltdowns, and all kinds of emotions. So, I'm going to go back to around the age of 1 years old and take it from there.

I had a good vocabulary for my age, I was fully potty trained by 18 months old. I didn't have a dummy for long either; my parents had stopped me having one when I started my potty-training. I was a good eater; I would eat whatever was put in front of me. I was an easy-going child up until the answer **NO** was introduced to me, then the temper tantrums kicked in. I would go crazy, I would **STAMP** my feet hard as I can, shout and scream at the top of my lungs until I got my own way.

Around about the age of 2½ years old, I started nursery for 2 half days a week. My mum was told regularly that I would choose to play on my own, away from the other children. However, I was attached to the nursery teachers all day; I would much prefer to be with the nursery teachers than kids my own age. I wouldn't make friends naturally; it was an Impossible task. My social skills were below average for my age, I didn't know how to approach the other children; I would be bossy and overpowering. I would be very loud when talking and playing and I would refuse to take  naps; I wouldn't settle at all. I wouldn't sit still to listen to a story, and I had absolutely no interest in listening to books. I wouldn't sit down for quiet time with the other children, I had to be doing something practical and I always had to make everything louder than it needed to be. I was terrible at sharing and there was no reasoning with me. If I didn't agree with you, I wouldn't listen; it was as simple as that. I wasn't really invited to any birthday parties either.

From 2½ years old my behaviour at home was starting to become an issue for my parents, because of this I was given the nickname of **MOODY MOLLY**. I would be extremely demanding; I had a strong stubborn attitude; it was either my way or no way. I didn't like doing things on my own I had to have 1-1 attention all the time with my parents. I was constantly running around being boisterous. I was really clumsy. I would scuff my shoes without meaning to. I was unnecessarily messy, and even the simplest task would still create a huge mess. I just didn't know how to do things quietly, carefully, or gently. My parents described me as being heavy handed. I was getting more and more stroppy and demanding as I was getting older, but my mum said I was always a very affectionate little girl. I would always say I loved her, and I was always kind and caring about my family. Although, when I wasn't getting my own way everybody knew about it.

The **BIGGEST** problem with me as a young toddler was my sleeping. I refused to sleep anywhere but next to my mum. I wouldn't fall asleep unless I was with my mum. My parents had decorated my room many times trying to make it easier for me sleep in, but it just never happened. My parents decided to consult a child sleep therapist to try and help them. But whatever they were trying just wasn't working. I wouldn't sleep in my own room. I had to sleep in my mums' bed. There wasn't anything they tried that was successful.

Eventually my parents were told that I would eventually grow out of it. I wasn't harming either my parents or myself, so they were advised to just let it take its natural course. They would rather me be happy and content than going to sleep distressed every night. But I never did just grow out of it. It continues to be a problem now. I was emotionally attached to my mum, I hated leaving her. She was and is my comfort zone. I couldn't settle unless I was with her. We tried many strategies like assisted sleeping until I fell asleep, reward systems, stickers. Nothing helped. I just didn't like sleeping without my mum. My dad was sleeping on the sofa in the living room permanently. He was such a trooper because he did that for **ME**.

My parents described me as a tomboy, I wanted all the boy things my cousin H had. He played in a football team, so I wanted to. He wore a tracksuit, so I wanted to wear a tracksuit. He had a toy car, so I wanted a toy car. I craved his attention too all the time. I would come across as very "in your face" and bossy. I would snatch his toys, push, and shove him. I just wanted to be his friend, but he wasn't having any of it. I would happily play in the mud and get all mucky. I was **GO GO GO -** and boisterous. I was always looking for attention from someone. I had to have some attention, whether good or bad at all times.

Around the age of 3, I was starting to be much more of a handful. My behaviour was becoming more challenging. I was having more frequent tantrums. I wouldn't take **NO** for an answer. I would push people's  buttons because I knew eventually, I would get my way. I had become very hyperactive, and super-strong willed. Again, accepting **NO** for an answer was the biggest issue at this age. I was very impulsive, if I wanted something, I wanted it **NOW!** I would always break my toys, from being too heavy handed with them.

My relationship with my dad was very strained. We were always arguing. He couldn't handle my mood swings and tantrums. He did everything he could to make me happy, but for some reason I never truly appreciated him. I only ever wanted to be with my mum. I didn't want anyone but my mum. I would only settle with her around me, I would always want to be cuddling her, she was like my comfort blanket. I definitely suffered with some form of emotional attachment issue. My dad has said that it was a very hard time, as he felt unwanted and useless, he just couldn't seem to bond with me easily.

Not only was I a **MUMMYS GIRL**, but I was also very close to my **NANNY**. We had an amazing relationship. She was a beautiful woman, inside and out. She had that stereotypical grandma look. Beautiful rosy cheeks, with Curly burgundy hair. She was the other person in my life that I totally adored. She was my world.

My grandad was also always around, he was very much in the background though. He loves the football, and he would watch football all day, every day. My nan was much more of a hand's on grandparent. I have always been brought up in a strong family unit. I had 2 aunts, 1 uncle and 2 male cousins. I was a very fortunate little girl, to have been blessed with such a strong family support system.

I liked my sandwiches cut in rectangles, otherwise I wouldn't eat them. I would have a complete meltdown if I was brought a sandwich that was cut any differently. I hated anything that had to go over my head for example, dresses without a zip. I hated feeling trapped.

I've always been petrified of lifts. **NOW GUYS** ... you're going to laugh at this one, but honestly it was a huge issue for me not only in childhood but it's still an issue now, I wouldn't wear socks. I wouldn't touch them. They made me physically sick. There was just something revolting about them.

If I had to wear socks, I would need my eyes covered and someone else putting them on my feet for me. They felt crusty after being washed, the horrible seam inside the sock would annoy me so much. I would need a brand-new pair of socks for each day. I have never gotten over this. I still don't wear socks and if I have to, I will buy new pairs and throw them straight out after I've worn them.

I couldn't wear certain t shirts; I would have major meltdowns if I felt like the T-shirt was **ITCHY** and **PRICKLY**.

When I was just getting to the age of about 4, and I was about to start infant school. I can remember going around my nan and grandad's house to play **SHOPS**. This is honestly the best memory I have of both of my grandparents. My nan was unable to walk due to a stroke and only having one leg.

So, myself and my grandad used to ask my nan for a shopping list, then we would go into their kitchen  cupboards, and take out all the cans. We would play for hours just pretending to scan all the food in the kitchen on my toy till. The reason I'm telling you this is because I could never play with another child the way I played with my grandparents, I couldn't connect with other children.

I was always happy and content playing alone at nursery away from the other children. But when I was with adults I would engage fully and really enjoy their company; I would be a totally different child. My imagination was very wild, I could play make believe better than playing real life games, based around me or my life. I wouldn't engage in games where I wasn't able to use imaginary play. I liked to make up characters and pretend to be someone else.

So, to put it bluntly, I wasn't exactly the world's easiest child. I had to over-come challenges even when I was as young as 4. It was the start of a very confusing and difficult life ahead. But thankfully I had the best parents by my side for the whole journey.

My toddler years were the best. My childhood has always been one of the happiest periods of my life. Although each year came with its own troubles, difficulties, and challenges. But I didn't have any "label" so, myself and my family just **GOT ON WITH IT**. My life was always "Normal" as my parents didn't ever treat me differently. They never made me aware that I had differences. They loved me for who I was, and they love me for who I am now!

A summary of some of my toddler life experiences, that I struggled with:

- Attachments issues.
- Understanding social situations.
- Understanding the importance of sharing.
- Making friends.

- Engaging in group activities.
- Engaging in conversations with other children.
- Learning to socialise.
- Accepting NO for answer

I was lucky enough to have an incredibly kind and supportive family to guide me through my struggles. I had a hard time when things changed, I didn't like the fact, I was no longer in control. I didn't ever feel **ALONE**, because I had a family full of beautiful, supportive people who loved me unconditionally.

These are some very special photos from when I was in my element, in the company of one of my best friends: **MY NANNY FRUIT BAT**.

# MY JOURNEY
## THROUGH EDUCATION

I left school back in 2014.

Who would have thought that the trouble I now call **ADHD MAYHEM** would end up getting even more challenging and chaotic at college? I was eventually kicked out of college and that was the point where I knew there was something not quite right with me.

Honestly, it was one of the scariest things I have ever had to do. It took **A LOT** of guts for me to approach my parents with my concerns. I felt like it was going to be embarrassing, admitting that I wasn't **NORMAL**; I was allowing myself to become extremely vulnerable.

But 2 years **LATER ...** and a LONG NHS waiting list ... and a private consultation later ... and **many, MANY** more issues with work and friendships ... **I, finally at the age of 21 received my diagnosis of ADHD.**

Surprisingly, my only reaction was to burst out crying.

**FINALLY,** I had an answer to why I wasn't like everyone else. But the challenges and problems didn't stop there. A new chapter of my life had only just begun and I'm so happy, that you guys have decided to read my journey.

**ADHD is a tough condition to suffer from but honestly, I'm sure, we can all smash**

**life and give it our best shot ... We got this my fellow ADHD'ERS.**

**BUT,** now for the school life gossip you guys and gals have come here for.

Just before I start showing you my reports, I want you to know that I can now look back now and laugh at these, but it has only just become **ACCEPTABLE** to talk about it in my house. Haha.

I can now understand why I acted like this, **BUT** I don't condone this behaviour for anyone reading this. If you are at the age where you're at school, and you might still be in that phase of wanting to annoy the teachers. **I DON'T CONDONE THIS AT ALL.**

I'm just showing you guys this as I want to give you a true insight into my journey growing up undiagnosed and struggling in school. I feel like it could potentially give the parents on here some hope and comfort. I hope to make you laugh even just a little bit as some of the things I got up to are funny.

**My behaviour has always been challenging.**

My parents said that throughout my life I have always displayed challenging behaviour. I have always wanted everything my way otherwise I would have a huge **MELTDOWN**.

**I've had to ask my parents for some help with this bit.**

**Things I can remember about primary and infant school:**

**Friendships** - Have always been a **HUGE** struggle for me. If I had a friend, I would make them feel like they weren't allowed to have any other friends. If they had other friends, I would feel betrayed and heartbroken. I was very jealous. As I've grown up, I've become more aware that the reason behind this is that I know/believe I'm easily replaced. I know that it will probably ... always happen. I'm always the second choice or the one that gets left out. It got to the point where I'm used to it now and I don't bother trying to make friends.

**Separation anxiety** - From my mum, is and always will be a huge issue for me. I will never feel safe unless my mum is by my side. It's like I always think something is wrong or something bad is going to happen to me. Then, it kick-starts my general anxiety disorder. It's a never-ending cycle for me.

**Lying** - Has always been an issue and it's something that I still struggle with now. It's not lying about things; it's lying about who I am. I lie to try and fit in. I'm almost like a Chameleon, I can change personalities to adapt to whoever I'm with, just like chameleons change colours to hide from their predators. I use the coping mechanism of **MASKING** to help cope with my issues around not fitting in.

**Not being academically gifted** - Never helped with my behaviour. I always felt like I was miles behind everyone else. I would act up to hide the fact that I was academically struggling. Boredom was a **HUGE** problem for me. I never had much interest in any of my school subjects. The only ones that I ever had any interest in were photography and graphic design. If I was in a lesson with a group of kids that I considered were my friends, I would keep playing up to make them laugh.

Anyway, trust me when I say there were many more!

I would be here for hours writing them down, but these were the ones that affected me the most.

When I got to secondary school **YEAR 7** something just clicked. I started to notice myself becoming angrier and more upset. I started to become more Isolated. I have never felt like I fitted in. I went from friendship to friendship, and the outcome was always the same. It ended up with bitchy squabbling and things getting way out of hand. Other than that, I wasn't "naughty" it was just friendships were my issues. I was, however, disorganised, forgetful, and **LOUD**.

**YEAR 8** was the year I started to get involved in things that lead to my behaviour getting serious.

*I was*:
- Walking out of lessons.
- Running around the school; running the teachers ragged.
- Not showing up to lessons/assembly.
- Eating in lessons/throwing food around classrooms.
- Wearing the incorrect uniform on purpose i.e., hoodies/ jeans.
- Fizzy drinks were banned but guess what … **I BROUGHT THEM IN PURPOSELY**.

- Being extremely disrespectful to teachers and swearing.
- Attitude problems.

One of my worst behaviour experiences was when I was banned from school trips. I had been so badly behaved on a trip to London, walking off, doing what I wanted, then disappearing off to "*Cafe Nero*" when I should have been waiting for the coach. My friends at the time were just like me, they were mucking around in the theatre, shouting things out and throwing food. I was taken along with the other students back to the coach. Then I had to wait on the coach for the remainder of the trip.

On the way back home from London everyone had begun messing around and I had got involved, initially laughing, and then my friend took it too far and threw sweets at the coach driver. Well guess what? Because I was labelled as the "naughty" kid, I was automatically blamed and punished. I was banned from all school trips and clubs. **Nobody believed me when I said that I didn't do it.** I was just punished and from that day I had no respect for teachers, and It all got worse from there.

**YEARs 9/10/11:** Oh, my goodness. These were the **best and the worst days of my life.** I made some of the funniest memories I have made so far in my 21 years of life. **However, they were also the worst days and memories for both me and my family**.

-     I was excluded about 4 times within the space of 2 weeks. This was becoming increasingly frequent as the years went on.
-     I was put in the local pupil referral unit.
-     I was badly bullied.
-     I was suicidal.
-     I became unbelievably nasty to my parents.

- I lost any motivation to do well in school.
- I lost sight of the police career I wanted back then.
- I squared up to my deputy headteacher.
- I got involved with the wrong crowd of people.
- My anxiety became an even bigger issue.
- I just did what I wanted.
- I became a completely different version of myself.
- I swore at teachers.
- I caused vandalism around the school.
- I took away people's education from those that wanted to learn.
- I was constantly on my phone and getting it taken away from me.
- I would kick off a massive amount and cause a scene at school and out in public with my family. This would usually end up with me being restrained and excluded.
- I lost my mum and dads trust, and respect.

**I was always told that I was full of so much potential.** I just couldn't get myself to focus or to be even the slightest bit interested in trying.

The teachers tried to **CONVINCE** my parents throughout all of my school life to get me a diagnosis of ADHD or autism. My parents were well aware, that I had something wrong with my behaviour, but they just didn't want me labelled with it and not given the opportunities because of it, I should have.

To all the ADHD parents out there, try to listen, when the child tells you that they just can't help it. It's so true. I'm communicating for them when I say it's hard, we just need someone on our side for once.

We just need someone to believe us when we say that we can't help it. We honestly want the same things "normal' kids do. We just want to be liked and accepted. We just want to have fun. We have so much to give but so little understanding of our true selves. When we get the help and support, we need, we honestly can reach the stars. Patience, love, encouragement, and cuddles are all we want.

Just tell us that you believe us, and that you will help us sort it out. We will always have our troubles but they maybe not as many, with our teachers, carers, parents, and family by our sides.

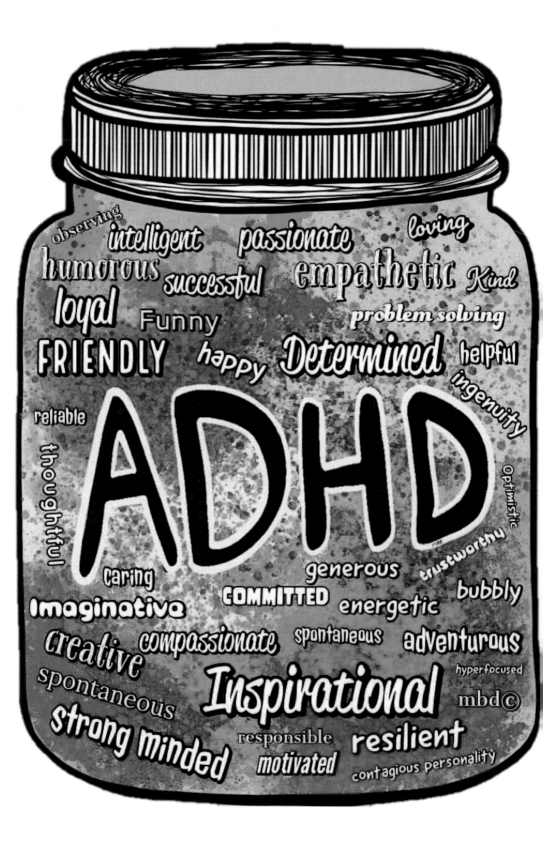

# TEACHERS ARE JUST AS IMPORTANT AS PARENTS...

So, before I start talking about my journey through education and my experiences with teachers, I want to give you an insight into my home life and my family life. This is going to give you a real insight into the world of **Me Myself and ADHD** ... **AKA** me, **MOLLY**.

Right so here we go ... We are going to start with my relationship with my parents and my sister. Remember I was only diagnosed in September of 2019. So, I've not been diagnosed for long, but I have had, suffered from, ADHD since I was about 2 or 3 and I haven't **GROWN OUT OF IT**. So, far it has carried on into adulthood. It's hard to talk about as it has affected my family massively, but all I can say is hang in there, it does get better guys! Honestly, it does. I'm living proof that it can get better, it just needs a little time and commitment and most importantly, you need your **FAMILY**.

As I was growing up, around the age of 5 or 6, I can remember the first time I understood what I had done, and how I had made my mum feel. I remember feeling pure hurt, heart break and disappointment coming from my mum. It was the first time I had ever had a "horrible thought" about my mum. I kept calling her names, and they were awful names. I feel sick even thinking about it now. Afterwards, I would feel so guilty and nasty every time I had one of those **HORRIBLE THOUGHTS**.

I would tell her that I wanted someone else to be my mum. I mean looking back at it now, I can't even imagine what was going through my head. I have the greatest mum in the world. She's my everything. She's the reason I'm still alive. I have nothing else to live for but her.

Anyway, like I was saying, from a very young age I wasn't exactly the golden child. This didn't change for a long time. I can remember it all as if it happened yesterday. It was the **HORRIBLE THOUGHTS** that I had which gave me such bad anxiety. It was like a being weighed down by guilt and a pressure which I could feel on my chest, all the time. If I didn't tell my mum what my horrible thought was, it was as if I would explode with the guilt, anxiety, and anger that had been suppressing me throughout the day.

I can remember one particular time when I had told my mum how I was feeling and had shared with her my horrible thoughts; every now and then I get flashbacks to this particular day. So, after I had finished telling my mum about my thoughts, I remember sitting in my "*groovy chick*" bedroom all alone, with my bottom lip doing that blubbering thing. I held in the sound of my crying, having just witnessed the colour disappear from my mum's face and tears fall from her eyes. I felt as though I had just murdered my mum; It felt as if I had physically hurt her.

Then, all of a sudden, my dad came in shouting at me, along with my grandad and aunt. They told me that my  mum was really hurt and that she didn't want to see me for the rest of the night. I can't tell you anything that could even closely represent the amount of pain I felt in that moment. My heart shattered. I didn't want to be thinking these horrific things about my mum. I wanted them to stop them, but I just couldn't. I felt like I was trapped in a someone else's head; someone horrible I didn't want to hurt my mum, and I had no idea why I couldn't stop thinking these horrible thoughts about her. Anyway, before this gets too long, I'll just say that my mum came around and collected me from my grandparent's house later that night. She told me that she forgave me, and I told her that I loved her dearly. I thought that was the end of all the nastiness inside my body. But NO! Things only got worse!

Well, I believe things got better for my mum. However, they got considerably worse for my dad and my sister. Things have never been **SUNSHINE AND RAINBOWS** between myself, my dad, and my sister but I guess things could always be worse, right?

Well let's talk about mine and my dad's relationship, shall we? I did have and I think always will have a hot temper. I think that's something that is going to be a problem forever. However, there have been times where my dad has literally smashed through my bedroom door because I'd barricaded myself in there by pushing my bed up against the door. There have been **MANY** times when I have physically assaulted my dad, punching, and kicking him but there are a few times that are particularly memorable. There was a time when I told my teachers and friends that my dad threw a hammer at my foot. It's funny to laugh at now but honestly, I don't know why I said anything like that.

**I GUESS IT WAS FOR SOME TYPE OF ATTENTION.**

I can just imagine the severe consequences of that silly impulsive lie.

There were many times that the arguments between myself and my dad EXPLODED and got out of hand. There was one time, in particular, that I grabbed a knife and threatened my dad with it before holding it up to my own throat. Things were getting **OUT OF CONTROL**.

I would tell my dad that I hoped he would die, or to go and commit suicide; this was on a daily basis. I have to admit that I wasn't a nice person, whatsoever. I'm deeply ashamed of myself for my behaviour; nothing good comes from violence. But it has a blessing to know that it's my ADHD. Having that diagnosis made things a lot easier for me to accept. I had pretty much accepted the fact that I was going to end up in prison, believing that I was a **CRAZY** psychopath.

Honestly, things inside my head were very messy. I had no idea it wasn't normal to think these awful things. I thought every child said things like this to their dads when they didn't get their own way. **NOPE I couldn't have been more wrong.**

Let's get down to the last person in my immediate family, my little sister, we are 4 years Apart. This is possibly one of the most upsetting things I have had to learn over the years and learning to accept it was even harder. I will openly say I **HAVE BEEN HORRIBLE** to my little sister. **VERY HORRIBLE - at that!**

**I see it now, and I also see the problems it caused between us.**

We don't have that "normal" sisterly bond. We never really have. I have always called her *"four eyes"* or *"freak."* I was awful towards her. I don't know what started it, but it just got worse and worse until one day, I came home from school and my sister had a been sent a card and a box of chocolates. It had been brought to her by this cute little friend of hers.
The card read:

> "To ...
> *I'm so sorry that your sister is horrible to you, I don't think you're a four eyed freak*
> *Love ...*"

I tell you what, it hurt. It hurt like hell. I can't say that it stopped it for long, but I didn't call her that particular name for a while. I was devastated that my sister had told her whole class, for **SHOW AND TELL**, that her older sister bullied her. I mean, what could honestly be worse than that? What was going on in my head? I remember this so clearly because I remember going upstairs and pinching both my thighs so hard with my nails to punish myself. I also remember lying about the bruises, and that I had done it to myself. It was because I was ashamed of who I was. I was such a horrible little girl, no wonder I had no friends.

It was a hard time for me. Please remember, at this point, I didn't know that I had ADHD. I didn't know ADHD even existed; all I can remember is the pain I felt in my heart. I still carry that feeling around with me now to this day.

My mum has told me on a few occasions while I was growing up that **my sister was scared to talk to me,** or **even look at me**. I mean, that's heart wrenching to know.

**It is a hard and very bitter PILL to swallow because no one should be treated the way I treated her or my parents.**

I'm not going to try and paint you a picture of how it's a perfect happy family now, because trust me, I'm still **VERY** hard work. I'm controlling, manipulative, aggressive and sometimes I'd go as far as **PURE EVIL**. Things have become easier in some ways, but in many other ways it's still the same.

***Mine and my dad's*** relationship has flourished since I have been on my ADHD medication. I can almost see the weight lifted from his shoulders, and he isn't constantly walking around in fear of my next **MELTDOWN**. We will always have our disagreements, but since having the official diagnosis of ADHD he has learnt to understand me more and it has done us both the world of good.

***Mine and my mum's*** relationship is like no other! She is the reason I live and breathe. She is my inspiration to get up in the mornings, because sometimes I feel as if there isn't anything worth living for but then I see my best friend's (my mum's) beautiful face, and I know that with her by my side I can achieve anything.

Finally, ***mine and my sister's:*** I personally believe that we now have the normal sibling relationship, but my ADHD adds a little more spice to it. I am very proud of who she is, and how strong and courageous she is. However, although I am happy, and proud of her, I  can't help but have this raging feeling of jealousy and hatred, not towards her as a person, but her life. I wish I could be her. I wish I could be free from ADHD. I want to be able to enjoy life like her, have boyfriends like her, have friends like her, have great career prospects, and more than anything be normal like her. When she goes out to parties, or other social events, I try my hardest to block out my negativity and be happy for her. I don't want to lie and say I just get over it and forget it because I don't. I get depressed and down in the dumps over it. I get jealous that she's only 17 and she is out having fun, and I'm 21 sat at home with my mum watching *"True Crimes."* It's like every time she achieves something; I can't physically be happy for her. It always turns into jealousy and hatred, for the situation not her. I take it out on her, because that's the only way I know how to communicate my emotions to her. I feel like I fail at being a big sister. I'm certainly no role model.

**SOMETIMES, I JUST WISH I WAS SOMEONE ELSE.**

I feel sorry for my family having to put up with me. It can't have been easy. I know just how tough it was ***fighting that battle in my mind alone for so long.*** **But I'm so thankful that now I have my diagnosis I can finally feel like there's an answer to my madness!**

**My journey through education -**

**SCHOOL** was a huge critical part of my growth. I definitely could have taken another path in life. I was offered drugs and alcohol all throughout my school life, but honestly, **I NEVER GAVE INTO THE DRUGS OFFER**, neither did I alcohol – although alcohol is a **WHOLE** different story: I was in photography class and as usual I was made to sit at the back of the room away from everyone; apparently, I distracted everyone from their work. One of my friends at the time, asked me if I wanted to try some of the **NEW "*RIBENA*"** and I was like 'There isn't a new flavour?' But she convinced me that there was, so I tried it and I **LOVED IT...** Then I started **ACTING FUNNY** ... and I felt funny, but I was clueless. I didn't understand why they were asking if I wanted more and more. It was like an endless bottle of *"Ribena."* Eventually I was told it was red wine ... Fortunately, I wasn't caught but it was funny! What, I'm trying to get at is, I'm easily led but the one thing I couldn't stand - was drugs.

**I'M SORRY MUM I KNOW YOU'RE READING THIS!!**

I hated disappointing my parents, especially my Mum. She is my biggest inspiration, I wouldn't be as strong as I am today, without her by my side. She is the reason I am the person I am today, but that would be too simple, and it wouldn't make the best story. So, I'm going to tell you about a couple of other people who have shaped me into the **WOMAN** I am today ... Sooo, let's get on with it.

Before we get into depth about my school life, I want to **INTRODUCE YOU TO MY ROLE MODELS**:

Obviously the first person who springs to mind ... My mum! Oh, my mum, doesn't realise how precious she truly is, she's a blessing to me and my family. My mum has the most beautiful soul and has the most beautiful face. If I turn out to be even a quarter of the mother she is, I will be well and truly blessed! My mum has fought against all odds and gets stronger each, and every day.

<u>My mum has</u> **Bipolar**.

I didn't know that until I was about 13 years old. That's right 13 years old. I couldn't even tell. She never used it as an excuse, and she never gave up on me to save her own mental health from suffering. She stayed **STRONG** to give me all the love and support I needed - I was always showered in love and support. There wasn't a day that went by that I had to ever question if my mum loved me. she is just one of a kind, and I'm thankful every day that I was/am blessed with her. I learnt this later in life, but honestly you should never take your mum for granted. She has taught me how to be strong, independent, and she has shown me what a good mother is. I have always known that I'm her priority.

But even though my mum was always my support throughout my school years our relationship was tested to the max!! There were several stand up arguments, silent treatment, and serious conversations between us. I needed someone else to lean on for support, and it was almost like my guardian angel had landed in human form. I was lucky enough to be given a mentor at school. For the sake of her privacy, I'm going to call her ***MRS M.***

***MRS M*** was my mentor, my go to person. She understood me more than I understood myself. I remember one specific day I was sat in her office. I looked up at her, and for some reason my heart instantly felt full. I was such a lost young schoolgirl, I had no friends, no future, and my family life was suffering at the hands of my challenging behaviour. I had a lot going on. I felt as though, I had the world on my shoulders but as soon as I was in MRS M's company, I felt content and safe. I knew that when I was with her, I didn't have to pretend to be someone I wasn't. I could let my guard down.

This is Mrs M ... **MY GUARDIAN ANGEL**.

This might sound strange to some people, but honestly, I was so alone and lost. I never had the privilege of having a Grandmother whilst growing up undiagnosed; my grandmother died when I was 7.

I didn't get to go and speak to my nan about my problems. I had no one. My parents were slowly giving up on me and I was turning into a monster.

**I had HIT that self-destruct button ...** Everything was falling apart around me **THANKS** to my behaviour.

I was becoming more and more distant from my family as my true ADHD colours were starting to become more vibrant. They weren't willing to put up with my behaviour for much longer. My bad temper and sudden outbursts were becoming a daily occurrence and along with my behavioural issues were becoming more and more difficult for my parents and teachers to cope with me. The only way I knew how to get the attention I was craving was to act up. My young mind was not being stimulated by the educational system and I was bored.

**My behaviour was at its absolute all time worst.**

I look back now, and I think about how obvious it was that I was lost and desperate for help. I was trapped in my own personal war within my mind. I didn't know how to fix it, but I saw **MRS M**, like a Grandma **FIGURE.** She always said it was just her job and she was just being a teacher, but I honestly needed the structure she gave me. I needed that type of support and guidance. She set me firm boundaries. I needed someone to be stern **BUT** kind, and I knew where I stood with her. I knew that whatever I did I could approach **MRS M** confidently enough to speak to **her** about it. Mrs M made me realise just how important a **TEACHER** is, and how much of an impact a supportive teacher can make on your life.

**This came in very helpful one Particular day.**

This particular day I had got myself into all sorts of trouble. I was going through so much with my home life, punishments, and consequences. Just like everyone else, I had hit my limit, I saw **RED,** and I was uncontrollable.

The police were already in my school, but they weren't **originally** there for me but then they were called to me. I wasn't in a good place at all. The police held me in the hallway, closed all the doors to stop other students coming in, until I stopped being a danger to myself or to others.

Unfortunately, even though the police had all the authority and were being extremely intimidating, I didn't listen to a word they said. I was doing what I wanted to do, as that was the mindset, I was in. I literally saw red. Then **MRS M** was called, and she then came in and spoke to me. I instantly became a lot less anxious and angry; I was back being my obnoxious, cheeky, and slightly arrogant self in no time.

I had so much respect for **MRS M**, and I hated shouting at her. I always knew where I stood with her, but that didn't always stop me from disrespecting her. Even then, I knew that she meant a lot to me. **I was pushing someone else away from me, that meant a lot to me; that was my only talent. The one and only thing I was good at.**

Year 9 quickly came around and I should have been getting ready to pick my options and extracurricular activities. Instead, I was getting ready to make even more mistakes and more serious ones than before, with even more consequences.

**So, I hope you're sat down comfortably with plenty of snacks, because trust me guys and gals, it only gets juicier from here on in...**

_**Year 9:**_ I had come back to school and had a new tutor whose name was **MISS W** (for privacy reasons I won't put her full name.) The chances of them reading this is pretty low, as I bet reliving the experiences, I put them through would give them a **BREAKDOWN.** She, Miss W, was only around 26 and I saw her vulnerability from a mile off. It was almost as if I was a sniffer dog for teachers' vulnerabilities.

Well, to put it bluntly my behaviour towards **MISS W**  was **VILE**. I would wind her up purposely, I would throw sweets across her classroom, deliberately aiming them at her. I would run out of the tutor and cause havoc. She was amazing with me, and she had honestly never done anything to deserve what I was putting her through.

One day, it all got a bit too much for me. **Miss W** was right by my side and she didn't leave until she knew that I was ok. I had put myself into some bad situations, but this one was the worst one so far.

**I had vandalised the school coach.**

I had run away from a school trip in London and caused a massive scene in the middle of London and inside the theatre. Then, I walked off and went to cafe Nero because I wanted a mocha. **My priorities were definitely in the wrong place!!**

I had started running around with some other out of control kids, and between us we managed to cause a lot of people a lot of stress. As a result, I was banned from every other school trip. I had to write a "sorry letter" to the theatre and coach company. I had only **just come back after a week exclusion**. I knew that deep down I had gone **WAY TOO** far this time. I was terrified about my parents finding out the **severity of the mayhem I'd caused.**

So, that day, I spent all day bunking classes. I was pleading with the teachers to not tell my parents. Well, I made things even worse believe it or not.

The events of that day are funny to look back on now, but at that moment in time it was like I was a **possessed evil hormonal teenage girl who didn't like admitting she was in the wrong. The events went like this:**

- I started the day off moody; anything I was asked to do was answered with a **NO**.

- I ended up going to PE and locking people in the changing rooms in the pitch black.

- I put people's clothes in the showers.

- I was banned from going inside at break times. I was meant to sit with a teacher, instead I decided I didn't want to. When they came to find me, I ran away, and when they asked for my report card and I ripped it up in front of them.

- I was rude to every teacher, swearing at them.

- Then, after 2nd break, I was not having any of it. I went back into PE, broke into the equipment cupboard, and started trashing the place. I threw balls at the ceiling and smashed the polystyrene tiles down. I even chased my friend around with a hockey stick covered in fox poo.

- Finally, I jumped the gate and got my PE shorts caught, so had to jump back over, denying all knowledge, despite having anti vandalism paint all over my PE kit. Plus, I had unintentionally given myself Rambo stripes on my face.

After lunch was when It really kicked off, I **mean REALLY KICKED OFF**, but before I start rambling on and trying to defend my actions. I have to introduce you to another **TWO** of my role models, firstly **MRS C**.

**Mrs C** was an **EXTREMELY** strict and firm teacher. She was the **DEPUTY HEAD TEACHER** and was in charge of maintaining the standards of the student's behaviour and their uniforms. Two things I wasn't great at.

**Matron**, well, all I can say about matron is that she made me feel content and secure whenever I 'graced' her with my presence.

**BELIEVE ME MRS C DIDN'T TAKE ANY S████!!!**

Right, so, after **ALL** the crazy Mayhem I had already caused throughout the whole day. Well, let's be honest the entire 3 years I had attended that school, I squared up to my deputy head teacher (Mrs C) ... But I'll rewind a little bit to give you the events that led up to this.

**MRS C** came to find me as she had heard that I was running riot. This resulted in her shouting at me; telling me she was getting my parents in and that I had taken it too far this time. So, I responded by backing her into a wall. Fortunately, the school nurse grabbed my fists just as I was about to swing; I was raging with pure hatred and anger at **MYSELF**. **Matron** came to my rescue, took a hold of my hands, pulled me aside and tried to calm me down. I knew my parents were going to be disappointed, so, I aggressively pushed my chair back, got up and walked off.

I violently shoved passed **MRS C** and took off on one of my many **Teenage "tantrums."**

The one time I needed someone, it was my new Tutor, **MRS W (who by the way I also treated like s███)** was the only one that stuck by me. She made several efforts to reason with me and made time to listen to me. She often agreed with me and she didn't shout or get angry at me. Mrs W was not sugar coating the situation or lying to make me feel better; she simply respected me enough to tell me the truth. We spoke about the mayhem and madness of that day and about what triggered my behaviour. I told her I had messed up and I was scared about my parents finding out. In turn I respected her for her honesty. She didn't just sit there and tell me that they wouldn't be mad; she told me that it was going to be hard. Thankfully, she reassured me that things get better and mistakes are what make you learn and grow into a better person. **MRS W went above and beyond to make sure I was OK**.

**She told me that she would be "right by my side the whole time."**

One thing though that she had said to me throughout  the whole conversation was, "Molly, in life no one is going to have your back as much as you have your own. You have to fight for yourself in the real world. School isn't anything like the real world.

The consequences of what you have done today, could have been very serious. You need to FIGHT for what you believe in by being passionate, but you need to learn that whatever you **CHOOSE** to do is **down** to **YOU**. **YOU** make the decisions, and you have to take the **consequences**, whether it is wrong or right. If you **BELIEVE** in **YOURSELF** and **LOVE YOURSELF,** you won't **EVER** let yourself down. You need to remember every **CHOICE** you make has a **different consequence** and you have to be prepared to take responsibility for your **CHOICES**. Everyone sees things from different perspectives / angles. You might be innocently having a laugh, but someone else could be offended by your actions, so **THINK** about your actions before you do them. Think about the impact that it could potentially have on someone's life, year, month, week, or day. Just imagine you we're stood on top of a cube, and you had 3 other people stood around the cube watching the **EXACT SAME** incident. You would assume that you would all see the same thing, right? **YOU'RE WRONG!** ... You will never see it how the other 3 people see it; you all have different points of view. You aren't always going to agree with other's opinions or decisions, but you have to remember everyone sees things differently. Everyone, deserves the chance to explain their point of view!"

*This has stuck by Me, even up to this day. It's very true, and because of this, she has also had an impact on my life ...*

Sadly, the teacher I squared up to, was my Mentor, **MRS C** and so, she had absolutely no choice **BUT** to forgive me. Mrs C was an incredible teacher, forgiving and caring, but with an equal helping of stubbornness.

She stuck by me and fought for me to be given another chance, every single time I messed up **(TRUST ME THERE WERE MANY MORE TO COME).** Amazingly she **NEVER GAVE UP ON ME**.

How lucky was I?

I had Mrs M, Mrs C and Mrs W, all willing to help me through secondary school. They were **ALL** individually willing to help and support me. **BUT**, most importantly they were willing to believe in me when everyone else was giving up on me. They had all spoken to me separately many times about my behaviour and the importance of my grades. I was on report card after report card. I had been on break and lunch time suspensions, detentions, and exclusions. Nothing was working. They were beginning to run out of ideas on how to help me.

But nothing could have Prepared them for the **TRAUMATIC and STRESSFUL** experiences, my behaviour had in store for all of us during the last few years of my school life; my undiagnosed ADHD really knew how to shake things up and make things more entertaining!

*I know you're probably reading this thinking I'm over exaggerating but believe me I'm not …*

There's one day that I can remember as if it was yesterday. It can't have been much longer after the previous incident I shared with you. My behaviour was in no way any better; if I'm being honest it was **much worse** than it had ever been.

If I remember correctly, I was only allowed into school part time. I was also put into a pupil referral unit part time and when I was in school, I was only allowed in half of the school building. I wasn't allowed to roam the corridors and I had to be escorted to each lesson; even my break/lunch times were taken from me. I was basically in **PRISON.**

During my only **FULL DAY** at school, I was told that I needed to go to the mandatory assembly. I never usually went to assembly; I hate feeling like I was trapped. **My teachers didn't know about my anxiety at this time.** They weren't aware of the **severity** of **the panic attacks that** I was experiencing every night and even throughout the day. **I would usually just get up and walk out of lesson when I was suddenly hit by my anxiety**. This generally happened when I was isolated or away from my friends, although I was in a tutor group with my friends on this occasion. I lined up accordingly and I was quiet because I was very conscious of the fact that I was being watched by the headteacher and my mentors.

When we got into the assembly hall, I slyly ran to the back of the line so I could sit next to my friends. Surprisingly, I wasn't caught as my quiet is still very **LOUD** so, I thought I had got away with it. I cockily strutted to my seat when I realised my mentor **MRS C** was watching from afar. She pulled me out and sat me at the back where I was supposed to be - on my own.

*Well, ... this is where it gets crazy ...*

**TWO OF MY** mentors were presenting the assembly. They were both preoccupied, so I snuck back to sit with my friends, I wasn't caught this time, so it was all good.

I pulled out my phone and started scrolling through my social media platforms. My tutor **MRS W** made those crazy eye movements that teachers make before creeping up behind me and grabbing my phone. I immediately stood up and started shouting at her. I was sent out, but I **NEEDED** to **LISTEN** to the assembly, so eventually I was allowed back.

**Well, guys and gals, this assembly was just about to get surprisingly exciting. Hold on to your seats, this is about to get slightly interestingly eventful.**

The assembly was about the expectations of the student's behaviours, punctuality to lessons and attitude to school in general. It started with the slide show of the boring "rules" like:

- No swearing.
- No fighting/violence.
- No Mobile phones allowed out during the school times.
- No running in corridors.

**You know the basic boring stuff ...**

Then MRS M started reading names from a list. **I THOUGHT** it was all the **good kids** being called out for being **PERFECT**. I noticed that MRS C was making her way towards the main exit from the hall, which leads to the head teacher's office. I was convinced that the **good kids** were going to get awarded and I was ready to crack open my packet of Haribo, and have myself a solo party, but before I could ...

**My name was called out ... (ohhhh dear) ... I was like, I'm not a good kid. Am I?**

**ABSOLUTELY NOT IS THE ANSWER TO THAT WITHOUT A DOUBT.**

I was really confused. So, I politely asked what they wanted me for? They didn't reply the first time, so I refused to get up. So, they both rapidly moved towards me. They whispered to me from the end of the line of seats; I was sat on the 5th or 6th seat in. I was pretty much smack bang in the middle. They both said, in a synchronised format, 'Molly don't cause a scene.'

So, I swiftly put my headphones in and ignored them. Both mentors, and the head teacher tried physically moving me by trying to move my chair, tugging at my blazer. All of which was intended to influence me into "making the right choices." **This was followed by most of the teachers pretty much surrounding me**. I was obviously trying my hardest to ignore and refuse them, as I was not being humiliated in-front of every single student in the school.

I asked them once again what their reasoning was behind asking me to stand up in assembly, as I couldn't think of one thing that was necessary. They answered with,

**'Ok, stay there and we will deal with this after, Miss Brooks.'**

I was really irritated; I hated all the drama and attention they had focussed on me.

My **anxiety** was beginning to kick in. My **adrenaline** kicked in along with my **fight or flight mechanism**. I could feel a **panic attack brewing**. My **legs and hands started to become numb, the room around me felt**

**like it was becoming smaller and caving in on me**, I was so good at **masking** it that **NOBODY** would have known.

They continued to call out the names of the children they wanted to stand up at the front of the hall while I carried on freaking out in my mind; silently screaming. I was afraid my panic attack would become strong enough to overwhelm me in front of **EVERYONE**.

I had no proper techniques in place to help with my panic disorder. I had learnt to resort to pinching my thighs and neck to focus on the pain and take my mind off my panic attack.

**This was my first panic attack in public, and in school too. It was also the first one I had experienced while I was away from my mum.**

I was pinching myself so hard to that my eyes were watering. I had my hoodie on under my blazer which was not allowed, but I wore it anyway. I put my hood up and put my music on loudly, to try and drown out my anxiety and my overwhelming desire to drop to the floor and scream for my mum. I turned my music down once I noticed the students walking towards the exit. The teachers finally got to the last student and then one of them said:

**'The reason we have called you lot here is because you don't behave. You aren't representing our core behaviour values and we wanted to let everyone**

**know who it is that is bringing down the score of our school's overall behaviour; it is only a small amount of pupils letting their year groups down.'**

**GUESS WHAT HAPPENED ... Yes, you're right ... I BLEW UP!!!!**

I got up and was heading straight to the front of the assembly to confront them. I wasn't happy that my name was being attached to something extremely personal and humiliating. I was taken out of the assembly hall and I was told 'you have pushed it too far this time Miss Brooks' I turned around and replied with,

**'I obviously haven't pushed you F CENSORED hard enough because you're still standing and annoying me**.'

Well let's just say I was excluded that day. I was told that I might not be welcome back at all. I honestly thought that I wouldn't make it into year 10. I thought I had ruined my chances of being a "better daughter" or "better student."

Whilst I was waiting, I told the school nurse that I didn't want to be here anymore, and that I didn't want to be myself anymore. I was convinced my actions were justified, because of the amount of humiliation I had felt. Deep down I knew I had mucked up. I was so disappointed that I let myself react like that.

I had an awful relationship with my parents at this point. I felt so alone and scared. I remember googling **"WHAT IS WRONG WITH ME?"** while sat waiting for my parents to pick me up. I knew that there was no way of fixing it this time or even sweet talking my way out of it.

Unknown to me the police were called in for this meeting. My mum and Dad walked straight past me without even acknowledging I was at there. They were called into the meeting while I was made to wait outside. Shockingly, my dad came and grabbed me pushing me into the meeting room, and because I wouldn't apologise, he grabbed hold of me and shouted in my face. He too, was very angry and humiliated.

The police officers took me away from the meeting. I could hear my mum and dad say, 'take her to social services, we can't have her anymore.' I burst out crying. Everyone was staring through the windows. They all saw me marched out of the school by the officers.

Realistically, I was only being taken to the police car to be out of the way for the duration of the meeting. It was getting out of control. My parents were talking about putting me into **CARE** ... I thought I was going to be the next *"Tracy Beaker."*

I was taken back in and because he had grabbed and shouted at me my dad was officially banned from the school. He wasn't allowed on the school property and was kicked off the school property. I had caused a lot of trouble that day, but the pain and heartache that I had caused myself was even worse. I was eventually allowed back to school a week later.

I came to find out that the only reason I was allowed back was because both my mentors, had put their faith in me, and they made me promise that I was going to try. I didn't, I messed up that day and was excluded again.

This time it was for good, I was only allowed in for maths and English lessons and for my exams. I had to go to the pupil referral unit and had weekly meetings with my teachers to catch up on the work.

I want the parents to know that I'm here if you want advice, I know how stressful it must be. My mum is always available in the group for a chat, (referenced in the front of this book.) She went through all of this and she would be willing to help you guys out or write a post if you wanted her to.

Anyway, I have **4 STRONG** women that inspired me to become the person I am today. I have never been made to feel different, I've always been encouraged. I'm very lucky to have had those teachers towards the end of my school life. I wish I'd had them since year 7. You never know what amazing things could come from having supportive teachers. They all inspired me in different ways. It's so important, to have a support system!

**IT MAKES LIFE A LOT EASIER HAVING SOMEONE ON YOUR SIDE.**

This is a true representation of a normal day in the life of Molly brooks:

I was regularly sent to MRS M.

This is me and Matron; we got on great!

# FRIENDSHIPS/PRESSURE TO BE "POPULAR"/MASKING MY STRUGGLE WITH "BAD BEHAVIOUR" TO GET THE ATTENTION I WAS CRAVING.

Being a teenager or a young adult without any mental health issues comes with its own set of personal battles and problems. For example, things like being extra moody and hormonal plus huge amounts of peer pressure. My generation also has to cope with the pressure to look like the "perfect" models on social media. We equally feel as though we aren't worthy if we don't achieve that perfect "career."

We expect ourselves to have our lives perfectly mapped out before we even turn 25. It can leave us feeling that we aren't successful or aren't ever going to be successful.

Peer pressure can be a real challenge for youngsters, it can lead to really serious consequences. I've never understood why some people honestly believe things like: **You need to do drugs, or drink to fit in with the COOL crowd at school/college.** I just don't understand why people would go out of their way to purposely make others feel **SO** inadequate. It can be something as small and petty as not having the most up to date mobile phone, or because you aren't doing the same things as your peer group.

I find it really difficult to believe that I gave in to some of those peer pressures. These days, I see myself as a stubborn strong young woman now and looking back I can't believe that I actually believed that rubbish.

It's so **CRAZY** to think that popularity and likability can make you do things that you know are morally wrong and go against all of your own beliefs and self-respect. Sadly, not everyone can just walk away from peer pressure.

Young people with or without ADHD, have to deal with peer pressure and it's hard to decline offers when you so desperately want to **FIT IN** or be in that **POPULAR** group at school. You end up believing that you will gain popularity from doing those things. They are usually things that you wouldn't ever have dreamed of saying yes to, but you get so caught up in the idea of becoming popular.

All that aside, there is something **extra**-ordinary about mixing ADHD and anxiety with the **NORMAL** teenage/young people hormones. It can create **HUGE** problems at home, at school and/or outside of school. Unfortunately for me, I found myself getting into all these strange scenarios both at school and college.

As you know, my life has been a massive personal struggle, but it's also been one hell of a journey with some unforgettable experiences. I wouldn't ever want to change a single part of it because it has made me who I am today, along with support and guidance from some very **INSPIRATIONAL WOMEN** that I was lucky enough to have had in my life.

**Here's a recap of my 'undiagnosed' ADHD traits, when I was at school that I struggled with** - bearing

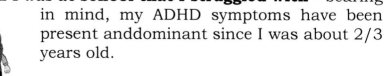

in mind, my ADHD symptoms have been present anddominant since I was about 2/3 years old.

- I have never had any long-term friendships.

- I used to always feel that I needed to lie about who I actually was in order to fit in.

- There are only very few people in the world who know the real "Molly."

- I would **PLAY UP** in class because I desired some/any attention from my peers, because I just wasn't "fitting in." This was evident from such a young age. As a result of my ADHD, I have always set myself unrealistic expectations.

- I would try and make myself believe that I needed to change who I am in order to make friends. As I got older (12-13) it became apparent to me that "no one liked me" - I was never invited to parties, I was always the one that was left out of a group.

- I just never felt like I fitted in anywhere.

So, with these extra little problems I had to deal with the fact that I was also undiagnosed and struggling to understand what I was doing to be so unlikable. With all of this happening in my own little mind, my behaviour went downhill from about 12 years old.

Because I knew I wasn't popular, I started craving attention whether good or bad; I just wanted attention from someone - **CONSTANTLY**. Don't get me wrong, I still don't understand why people don't like me now. It hasn't got easier, but over time you I have become more used to it and started to accept it. I would still do nearly anything to be classed as someone's friend.

In many cases I was just going along with things to get that satisfaction, even if it only lasted a short time, it made me feel wanted.

The pressure of good grades never phased me. I was never bothered by anything to do with grades. I knew I wasn't going to be a doctor so in my mind I just accepted that I was dumb. I was always trying to be someone I'm not by doing things like -

• Being loud. I would be loud, like I was laughing into a megaphone.

• I would always be argumentative with teachers.

• I would mask the fact I'm hurting and struggling, by being obnoxious and sarcastic towards the teachers.

I knew it was wrong, but like I said I just needed the attention from anyone who would give it to me. I soon learnt that the fastest way of getting attention was by playing up and misbehaving. This **ATTENTION** became an addiction in the sense, that I just couldn't get enough.

I preferred getting bad attention because it lasted longer than just getting a **WELL DONE**. The more I played up, the more attention I got. I would be on report which meant I would be known as the **NAUGHTY KID.** In my mind that was my identity; it made me feel like having that label made me untouchable.

Even the teachers just commenting on my uniform was enough of a fix to my addiction. I would then get in a **STRANGE** mood where

I just wanted to annoy teachers and cause a lot of trouble. I didn't know why I did it. I still don't know. I just did. I knew it was wrong, but I did it without caring about the consequences of my actions.

The threat of my parents being called began to be a daily occurrence, so it began to lose its importance. It was as though nothing I did satisfied my need to fit in and be the centre of attention.

Eventually I made a good group of friends in year 10, which lasted about 1½ years, I finally had that best friend and a great group of friends that were all very intelligent. I was like the cat that got the cream. I couldn't believe I was friends with these girls, but **BAM** I strike again! My behaviour had improved but it suddenly took a turn for the worse again.

I hated my **BEST FRIEND,** giving any of our other friends' attention, or even hanging out with them without me. I became this paranoid person who was obsessed with keeping **MY** best-friend. I became jealous, nasty, and eventually I ruined the whole friendship. I was the loner again.

After this I became friends with the younger year groups. I felt like I was the leader, all the younger students found me funny. I was like a **QUEEN** and I was finally getting that attention again.

**SOOO guess what happened?**

My behaviour got worse than it had ever been. The things I was doing were becoming more and more serious, until I was excluded for the first time. This almost became a weekly occurrence until the day I left. I was

moved part time to a local **PUPIL REFERRAL UNIT**. I knew I didn't belong there; I only wanted friendship and acceptance from people my own age. I had got myself into such a bad place and I couldn't get myself out of it; I had dug myself into a hole that was far too deep to ever get out of.

It was so bad that when I broke my wrist at school, one of my teachers didn't believe me and just thought I was mucking around. I had to beg them to believe me that I was **REALLY** hurt. I understood that I had acquired myself a horrible reputation.

**It was at this point I realised how far I'd taken things, and how much I had disappointed and pushed away the people that cared about me and my future.**

**COLLEGE**

**1ˢᵗ year** - The first few weeks I was a completely different person, listening and not interrupting. Doing my course work with a dedicated mindset, but it didn't take long before I was fed up with trying and reverted back to the old "Molly." I got myself into a lot of trouble with a group of people that were far from a great influence on me, **AT ALL**.

I was not turning up to maths, I started back chatting my teachers. I was acting just like I had at school, walking out, playing up, shouting, being argumentative or belittling the teachers in front of the  class. It gave me the feeling that I was still being back at school. I couldn't get myself into the college routine and I didn't get any attention from these teachers whatsoever. They knew all about my past, but they didn't care. I didn't get any of the special treatment I got at school and eventually after several warnings I was permanently excluded from classes.

I had to sit in an office with a behavioural teacher. I wasn't tolerated at college, but it had given me some attention, which was enough for the time being.

**2nd year - EVEN WORSE**, I was met on the first day by the teacher saying, 'I've been warned about you and I'll be keeping an eye on you.'

The first day I got the attention I was craving again, so in my mind I had to live up to that. It took me a few weeks, before I started walking out, not turning up, and doing what I wanted. I was just causing issues, not only in lessons but around the campus, kicking vending machines with **THE BOYS** and throwing stuff about. I was acting as If I was in primary school, and it was embarrassing for everyone. But I just didn't care. It was the only thing that gave me comfort. It's weird I know but I was like a baby with its blanket; it was my comforter. I didn't feel like I'd get through the day unless I got that attention.

### 3rd year - I WAS EVEN WORSE, AND I GOT KICKED OUT!!

It was a horrible time. I was 19 at this point and this was the point that I knew there was something wrong with me. I'm not normal and I'm not able to just act "normal for once."

I was 19, my classmates were 17/18 and I was acting as if I was 13. I caused havoc on a week-long college camping trip, to the point that my behaviour made the teachers

reach a decision that would make me see the reality of it all. They told me I would never get into the police with my behaviour as I had no respect for anyone, not even myself at this point. They kicked me out and I was devastated.

My whole world came crashing down, and I became aware of the awful reality. I was completely lost and felt like I didn't belong anywhere. I was depressed and I just didn't know what to do anymore. All I knew was how to cause drama and stress; I felt very uncomfortable with my life. I didn't want to live it anymore; it all became too much. I didn't believe there was ever going to be a light at the end of this harrowing tunnel for me.

**Fast forward 2 years** - I went to get a doctor's opinion on what was wrong with me; why I just couldn't be normal like everyone else my age? I just wanted to have friends, and a social life, but instead I was riddled with anxiety and depression. I just accepted that I would never have a friend. The GP referred me without any hesitation; she told me she was sure it was ADHD. It took **2 YEARS** on an NHS waiting list and even then, I had to go private to get a diagnosis of **social anxiety, generalised anxiety, and ADHD!**

Finally, I had an answer! There was a reason why I didn't fit in anywhere. I now knew why I just couldn't settle in anywhere.

Throughout my adult life, I have never fitted in at any

job I have had. I have had to leave every single one, because I always seem to find drama and it always becomes something more than it needs to be. I just can't seem to get things to work for me. I'm 21 years old

and I've had to leave 4 jobs. I am currently employed, and this is the longest one yet: 1½ years so far, don't get me wrong this one is far from perfect.

Nothing comes easily for me. Everything I do is always challenge.

I got myself into trouble with my car and driving license. I had to sell my car for my own safety and for the safety of others. I had no sense of fear. I would **SHOW OFF** because I finally had "friends," ... because I had a car. I later found out they totally used me; as soon as I got rid of my car, they weren't around anymore. This hit me hard, but I got through it and came out the other side because of my family.

**The hardest thing for me now after getting diagnosed is** - Comparing myself to others my age. Not having a boyfriend, or ever having a serious relationship is hard for me. I just can't seem to find anyone or even trust anyone; I'm a paranoid mess. Relationships can be dangerous with my ADHD as I become to obsessed. I can plan out my whole life with someone who gives me just a little bit of attention. I would do anything to be like the **NORMAL GIRLS** who have relationships. I see this as a milestone, which as yet I haven't completed, and I feel like a failure. I compare myself to anyone that I feel has what to me is the perfect life. I pick my life apart which starts off my impulsiveness and then I can't seem to stop myself being overwhelmed by my own thoughts.

- I get depressed about myself a lot.
- I hate who I am.
- I wish I was someone else.
- I just want to be like the girls my age that have perfect lives.

- My impulsiveness is a huge issue for me
- especially where my money is concerned; I don't take care of my savings or even my own bills.
- I am over generous I would give my last £1 if I thoughtI would make a friend over it.
- My emotions are intense.
- My anger and stress are just as intense.
- My ADHD **IS TOUGH**.

**IT IS NOT JUST A NAUGHTY KID ILLNESS!**
As I've got older my mental health has suffered, due to my ADHD being untreated for so long. ADHD comes with a lot of complex mental health issues. It doesn't just affect the person with ADHD either; it affects parents/siblings and grandparents etc. It has a ripple effect. As my sister has grown older, I have become jealous of her which has caused a rift between us. I so desperately want to be her, and I have a hard time accepting that she has a **BETTER LIFE** than I do. And although, I'm very proud of her, things just don't come naturally to me.

I just want people to know that those of us with ADHD so desperately want to be **ACCEPTED** and **SUPPORTED.** We just need a friend. We aren't that bad when you get to know us. We actually have amazing personalities; we are so caring and loving and we just want to give you the friendship we so desperately want.

If I could give some advice to someone that knows a person with ADHD, I would say – 'Just give them time, make them feel wanted, give them your attention, and be present in the moment; try not to be put off by our intensity.'

**We all just want to fit in!**

So, please parents and siblings of ADHD kids, or adults, just tell them that you love them and that you're proud of them! They would appreciate it so much. You will make their day. It's not often we get told that someone is proud of us!

**WE ARE AS PERFECT AS WE CAN BE.**

When you're with us we feel like we have a spine; that someone has our back. We just need you here with us every day, just for daily reminders and some comfort.

Thank you for choosing to read my journey and I hope you enjoyed it!

See you for the next one ...

**REFERENCES**

adhd-institute.com/burden-of-adhd/epidemiology/gender/
pinterest.com/amp/pediastaff/add-adhd/
attitudemag.com
chadd.org

The majority of research for this book was either through experience, or through asking questions of specialists during private therapy sessions.

| Name | Reg | Date | Incident | Description |
|---|---|---|---|---|
| BROOKS Molly | | 16 Feb 2011 | Monitoring Equipment Planner | No Planner |
| BROOKS Molly | | 16 Feb 2011 | L2 Repeat of the incident | |
| BROOKS Molly | | 21 Mar 2011 | Monitoring Equipment Planner | |
| BROOKS Molly | | 28 Mar 2011 | Monitoring Equipment Planner | |
| BROOKS Molly | | 01 Apr 2011 | Monitoring Equipment Planner | |
| BROOKS Molly | | 01 Apr 2011 | Monitoring Equipment Planner | |
| BROOKS Molly | | 03 May 2011 | Monitoring Equipment Planner | |
| BROOKS Molly | | 10 May 2011 | Monitoring Uniform Shoes/Trainers | |
| BROOKS Molly | | 01 Jul 2011 | Monitoring Equipment Pen | |
| BROOKS Molly | | 12 Jul 2011 | Monitoring Uniform Blazer | |
| BROOKS Molly | | 20 Jul 2011 | Monitoring Uniform Blazer | |
| BROOKS Molly | | 14 Sep 2011 | 'L1 Not considerate to others' | Stamped on a yoghurt pot during breaktime, resulting in another student's trousers getting very dirty. I did not see the incident as I was on duty elsewhere but there were student witnesses. |
| BROOKS Molly | | 15 Sep 2011 | 'L1 Not considerate to others' | Molly struggled to concentrate all lesson and tok every opportunity to distract others. Lunch detention set. |
| BROOKS Molly | | 22 Sep 2011 | 'L1 Not considerate to others' | Molly was heavily distracted during my lesson and dispite my attempts to get her to settle and stop calling out/talking/disrupting others. She continued to disrupt and twice made inappropriate comments about others in the group. Talked to at the end of the lesson and I will monitor next lesson. |
| BROOKS Molly | | 28 Sep 2011 | L2 Disruption of learning | |
| BROOKS Molly | | 06 Oct 2011 | L1 Using phone/ipod/headphones without permission | Continuesd to talk over me. Disruptive - I get so frustrated by Molly as she is a really nice girl and has never been nasty - I hope she responds when on report from next week. Some of te problem today was her continued calling out whe I had worked sor very hard to control and engage the group. Her points were valid, but she really needs to understand to put her hand up and wait until the teacher has finished. She can also get involved in silly little disruptive behaviours that need to stop. |
| BROOKS Molly | | 10 Oct 2011 | L1 Other Level 1 incidents | |
| BROOKS Molly | | 11 Oct 2011 | 'L2 Other minor incidents at teacher's discretion' | |
| BROOKS Molly | | 11 Oct 2011 | 'L3 Persistent disruptive behaviour (within lesson)' | Consantly talking throughout lesson, talking over peers and teacher. Very little |

| Name | | Date | Incident | Details |
|---|---|---|---|---|
| | | | | work, rarely on task. Extremely rude and blunt when talking to staff. |
| BROOKS Molly | | 13 Oct 2011 | 'L2 Persistent pre-level 1 breaches (same lesson)' | Decided to talk over me many times, warnings given with no effect. Then decided it was ok to drink in a science room. Molly is well aware that drinking is not allowed in a science room as I have to stop her doing it every lesson. Poor attitude to my lesson. Molly then had a quick meeting with Mrs Jones, returned with a very half harted apoligy and admitted that she couldent see what she had done wrong - this was then explained to her again. I like Molly but she has changed since last year. |
| BROOKS Molly | | 13 Oct 2011 | L2 Bringing fizzy/energy drinks into school | Molly spent the first half of the lesson refusing to engage in her work. In this period she consistently failed to stop looking at inappropriate websites when asked, refused to move seats and spoke rudely to staff when challenged. |
| BROOKS Molly | | 18 Oct 2011 | L2 Bringing fizzy/energy drinks into school | |
| BROOKS Molly | | 18 Oct 2011 | 'L3 Persistent disruptive behaviour (within lesson)' | extremely disruptive the whole lesson, minimal work, constantly talking over teacher/peers. Rude to staff when challenged. Kept throwing bits glue into Harmonie's hair. |
| BROOKS Molly | | 19 Oct 2011 | L1 Other Level 1 incidents | |
| BROOKS Molly | | 19 Oct 2011 | 'L2 Other minor incidents at teacher's discretion' | Caught eating twice in registration 30 min dt set |
| BROOKS Molly | | 19 Oct 2011 | L2 Bringing fizzy/energy drinks into school | No work |
| BROOKS Molly | | 20 Oct 2011 | 'L2 Persistent pre-level 1 breaches (same lesson)' | Continues to talk over me time and time again. Warned time and time again. Sent to another room to work. I am concerned that Molly can not see that her actions are why she is getting sent out. She will continue to defend herself in quite a calm way when being spoken to. I am very quickly running out of ideas to keep her attention in class. I taught Molly last year and she was great. Something has changed and she is nothing like she used to be. |
| BROOKS Molly | | 20 Oct 2011 | L2 Committing another incident in the same lesson | Told another pupil to 'fuck off'. |
| BROOKS Molly | | 03 Nov 2011 | 'L2 Throwing objects' | Molly repeatedly threw lumps of Pritstick around and at other students, causing damage to the classroom and Tameesha's blazer. |
| BROOKS Molly | | 08 Nov 2011 | L3 Other Level 3 incidents | Molly is incapable at present of acknowledging why she is a persistently disruptive student. She is unable to understand that every comment she makes in the lesson is tantamount to disruption of the lesson. This happens persistently and she eventually gets told off or removed from the lesson. This cannot go on and will be placed on inclusion next lesson. |
| BROOKS Molly | | 14 Nov 2011 | L1 Other Level 1 incidents | |

| | | | | |
|---|---|---|---|---|
| BROOKS Molly | | 14 Nov 2011 | L1 Using phone/ipod/headphones without permission | |
| BROOKS Molly | | 21 Nov 2011 | L1 Other Level 1 incidents | |
| BROOKS Molly | | 01 Dec 2011 | L1 Using phone/ipod/headphones without permission | Molly continued to talk over me - Detention set for lunch time today |
| BROOKS Molly | | 08 Dec 2011 | 'L1 Not considerate to others' | Molly was distracted very easily again today, and most of her problem is sniping comments to Jenna. I understand there may well be issues in this class with Jenna and Molly but is is disrupting my lesson at almost every chance they get! Molly did get better towards the end of the lesson - but the disruption caused too many issues. |
| BROOKS Molly | | 06 Jan 2012 | 'L1 Not considerate to others' | Molly continued to chat over me for the 2nd lesson in a row. This is nothing new and I now had no choice but to phone parents. When phoned the parents were supportive of the school. The father suggested that we may suspend her as she needs a real shock to get her back on track. We agreed that there should be a meeting to discuss her behaviour. A meeting between Miss Jones and Parents has been suggested - Miss Wilson no taking control of this situation. |
| BROOKS Molly | | 12 Jan 2012 | L1 Other Level 1 incidents | No planner |
| BROOKS Molly | | 13 Jan 2012 | L1 Lateness to lesson/tutor time | Repeated calling out followed by 'what the fuck...' Break DT. |
| BROOKS Molly | | 16 Jan 2012 | 'L1 No planner' | |
| BROOKS Molly | | 18 Jan 2012 | 'L1 No planner' | |
| BROOKS Molly | | 18 Jan 2012 | L1 Lack of or incorrect equipment/uniform/planner/PE kit | kept eating sweets, 10 mins break |
| BROOKS Molly | | 19 Jan 2012 | 'L1 No planner' | |
| BROOKS Molly | | 30 Jan 2012 | 'L1 No planner' | |
| BROOKS Molly | | 30 Jan 2012 | L1 Using phone/ipod/headphones without permission | eating, no work. 10mins dt |
| BROOKS Molly | | 30 Jan 2012 | L2 Bringing fizzy/energy drinks into school | Very negative and argumentative attitude. Refused to read. Detention set |
| BROOKS Molly | | 31 Jan 2012 | L2 Bringing fizzy/energy drinks into school | Molly was unable to stop talking, arguing and disrupting the lesson for more than a minute at a time. Came close to departental inclusion and BT detention issued. |
| BROOKS Molly | | 02 Feb 2012 | 'L1 No planner' | |
| BROOKS Molly | | 03 Feb 2012 | L1 Using phone/ipod/headphones without permission | thumping wall, taking photos of herself and peers in class. |
| BROOKS Molly | | 10 Feb 2012 | L2 Bringing fizzy/energy drinks into school | Molly stuggled to calm down and concentrate, calling out, falling off chair etc. Breaktime detention set. |
| BROOKS Molly | | 28 Mar 2012 | L1 Using phone/ipod/headphones without permission | Caught eating during registration then lied about it. 10 min DT set. |

| | | | | |
|---|---|---|---|---|
| BROOKS Molly | | 29 Mar 2012 | L1 Using phone/ipod/headphones without permission | Continued talking throught the lesson. Sent out for this and found it funny that she was. Poor attitude. Must improve for next term |
| BROOKS Molly | | 16 Apr 2012 | 'L1 No planner' | |
| BROOKS Molly | | 30 Apr 2012 | L1 Using phone/ipod/headphones without permission | Continued talking, a bit of work but not much! |
| BROOKS Molly | | 30 Apr 2012 | L3 Other Level 3 incidents | Refused to sit in alphabetical order in assembly. 1 hour school detention set. |
| BROOKS Molly | | 25 May 2012 | L4 Bullying (Physical) | Molly Brooks and 2 other students did not attend assembly and decided to goto the drama room to talk to a teacher. The teacher was under the impression from the girls that it was ok for them to be there, but in fact they had decided to do this off of their own backs. Molly Brooks actually lied to me and said that she had cleared it with Miss Wilson (Tutor). All to have a 1 hour Detention. Mr Orchard took them back to assembly. |
| BROOKS Molly | | 14 Jun 2012 | 'L3 Persistent disruptive behaviour (within lesson)' | Molly spent much of the lesson calling out, disrupting others and failing to follow even basic instructions. She moved table to be nearer Lily and Chelsea and had to be reminded to move several times. 30 DT set for 20th June. |
| BROOKS Molly | | 22 Jun 2012 | 'L2 Other minor incidents at teacher's discretion' | Molly and a friend were filling up water bombs in the toilet at breaktime. I confiscated them and warned the girls not to do anymore. Molly went to the staffroom and gave the rest of the packet to JW to avoid tempatation! Myself, DO and NB kept an eye on them throughout the rest of break. |
| BROOKS Molly | | 25 Jun 2012 | 'L2 Persistent pre-level 1 breaches (same lesson)' | Molly was over 5 mins late to the lesson and then continued to disrupt the other students in the class room for the whole of the lesson. I did ask her to leave the lesson and i then explained that she had to settle down but this did not appear to sink in. |
| BROOKS Molly | | 03 Jul 2012 | Witness | STATEMENT- Brandon Broad & brendan Westrope came up to Molly on the field & tried scaring her with their bikes. Brandon grabbed her bag with his foot & mollys phone fell out and hit the concrete which broke it. |
| BROOKS Molly | | 17 Jul 2012 | 'L3 Other more serious incidents at Curriculum Leader/Subject Leader discretion' | Molly thought it was ok to put chewing gum in Jenna McGarry's hair |
| BROOKS Molly | | 14 Sep 2012 | Level 1 | Molly refused to participate within the lesson |
| BROOKS Molly | | 20 Sep 2012 | Level 2 | refusing to take part in the lesson but after time and some negative language did take part. |
| BROOKS Molly | | 28 Sep 2012 | Level 1 | |
| BROOKS Molly | | 03 Oct 2012 | Level 3 | Refusing to take off gilet in school. |
| BROOKS Molly | | 10 Oct 2012 | Level 1 | Eating haribo in tutor time. Sweets removed. |

| | | | | |
|---|---|---|---|---|
| BROOKS Molly | | 15 Oct 2012 | Level 2 | Eating sweets and gum. Refusal to follow instructions to remove the gum. Sweets were taken and issue of gum was eventually dealt with. Molly was sent out to reflect on her defiance and for 5 mins. She was then kept behind at the end of the lesson into break to revisit expectations and rules. |
| BROOKS Molly | | 17 Oct 2012 | Level 1 | Eating haribo. Sweets confiscated. |
| BROOKS Molly | | 18 Oct 2012 | Level 3 | 3 lates inc prn |
| BROOKS Molly | | 24 Oct 2012 | Level 2 | On ipod in registration, asked her to put it away. She ignored me so I asked her to hand it over. She refused to hand it over. Eventually she gave it to CC. |
| BROOKS Molly | | 24 Oct 2012 | Level 1 | Caught Molly drinking fizzy drinks on two seperate occasions this morning. Removed both cans. |
| BROOKS Molly | | 25 Oct 2012 | Level 1 | Checked phone during video clip. Report card confiscated due to being covered in offensive language. |
| BROOKS Molly | | 08 Nov 2012 | Level 2 | tried to enter the room eating and continued to eat during the lesson even when asked not to. food was removed and molly told me to "chuck it in the bin i don't want them anymore". food binned but molly continued to moan about her food being taken away disrupting the lesson |
| BROOKS Molly | | 08 Nov 2012 | Level 2 | Refused to remove headphones after being told 3 times first by LM and VML. refused to stop talking and was moaning that she didnt like LM and wasn;t going to do anything she said. LM carried on introducing the controlled assessment and the disruption from Mollie continued , until it was unfair on the others VML removed Mollie to speak to VM and Mollie promised to not put headphones in and to do her work. |
| BROOKS Molly | | 09 Nov 2012 | Level 3 | Molly refused to participate within any aspect of the lesson. She tried to go back into the changing rooms to get her phone, came into the lesson saying 'im not doing it, i dont like circuits', then refused to put her hair up and to participate within any station of the circuit. Molly then distracted a number of students, trying to flick elastic bands. Molly wouldnt let me sign her report card as it would have been A5 P5. |
| BROOKS Molly | | 16 Nov 2012 | Level 2 | Persistent refusal to engage in the lesson, doodling on work, lolling across the table. Whenever we attempted to involve her in the discussions she repeatedly said she didn't care and that because she isn't a Jew it's pointless to talk about the Holocaust and no it doesn't bother her etc etc. She was taken for mentoring before the end of the lesson. A5/P5 on report. |
| BROOKS Molly | | 21 Nov 2012 | Level 1 | Disruptive behaviour - Talking |
| BROOKS Molly | | 22 Nov 2012 | Level 1 | Molly refused to let me sign her report card at the lesson. |

| | | | | |
|---|---|---|---|---|
| BROOKS Molly | | 22 Nov 2012 | Level 2 | |
| BROOKS Molly | | 26 Nov 2012 | Level 2 | refused to remove coat, sent out. asked again to remove coat, refused again. sent to complete test in another class |
| BROOKS Molly | | 29 Nov 2012 | Level 2 | Frequent attempts made by Molly to distract others through pulling faces and whispering. She also needed to be asked more than once to get rid of her chewing gum. She attempted to move within seating plan but returned to correct seat when asked. |
| BROOKS Molly | | 06 Dec 2012 | Level 3 | Throwing, eating, awful attitude to simple instructions. unable to follow instruction. Ran out of class with another students phone |
| BROOKS Molly | | 06 Dec 2012 | Level 1 | Found in main blocking at 2.05pm - when shouldl of been in Drama. I asked her why she was wondering and she walked passed me and shoiuted extremely loudly, Molly then walked off and would not follow simple instructions to come with me so I could escort her back to lesson |
| BROOKS Molly | | 10 Dec 2012 | Level 2 | Molly kicked the Basketball really hard during the lesson. I asked Molly to come over to speak to me, her reponse was 'oh, for gods sake' in a very rude manner. |
| BROOKS Molly | | 10 Jan 2013 | Level 2 | |
| BROOKS Molly | | 15 Jan 2013 | Level 3 | Absolutely no work completed, rude towards me, refuses to sit according to the seating plan and walked out of the lesson 5 minutes before the end. |
| BROOKS Molly | | 17 Jan 2013 | Level 3 | Failed to enter lesson - refused to do as asked. |
| BROOKS Molly | | 25 Jan 2013 | Level 3 | Absolutely no work, refused to put away chewing gum. |
| BROOKS Molly | | 28 Jan 2013 | Level 3 | constantly rude during the lesson and walked away at the end of the lesson when spoken to about this. Rang home and discussed with Mr Brooks |
| BROOKS Molly | | 04 Feb 2013 | Level 2 | continuously rude throughout the start of the lesson, heard her telling me to "shut up" but denied this. sent out |
| BROOKS Molly | | 14 Feb 2013 | Level 4 | Came in late to exam lesson, swearing and talking over everyone, major disruption to group. Then refused to do the work, walked out of class. After discussion with teacher and on call, returned to lesson and did minimal work. |
| BROOKS Molly | | 25 Feb 2013 | Level 4 | Refused to remove hoodie! Defiance of a teacher. |
| BROOKS Molly | | 04 Mar 2013 | Level 4 | Molly insisted on sitting on a table for 2 students that already had 2 students sitting at it. initially she moved as requested, but later in the lesson she moved back and refused to move. On call came up and she was eventually persuaded to move back to her correct seat. |
| BROOKS Molly | | 07 Mar 2013 | Level 4 | Molly very confrontational from the start of the lesson. Phone not put away etc. Then abruptly walked out of classroom. |

| | | | | |
|---|---|---|---|---|
| BROOKS Molly | | 30 Sep 2013 | L1 Other Level 1 incidents | Failing to do as told. Throwing a book. |
| BROOKS Molly | | 14 Oct 2013 | L4 Persistent refusal of an adults request | Molly 'sat out' of an activity where everyone was changing partners every minute telling me openly infront of another student that 'this is shit and I'm not going to do it. I hate it'. This was after repeated requests from me asking for her to join back in. I then spoke with Molly about the disproportionate amount of time that she was demanding/consuming. 'But I've told you I don't want to do it' was her response. Dept inclusion next PE lesson. RA informed. SAE informed as HOY. |
| BROOKS Molly | | 15 Oct 2013 | L1 not reading in ERIC | Not reading in ERIC and phone out. confiscated phone and still off task. |
| BROOKS Molly | | 25 Oct 2013 | L2 Disruption of learning | Constant use of mobile phone despite warnings and following of the behavioural policy. Molly refused to begin her work, constant refusal and rudeness towards me. VM arrived oncall. Molly apologised reluctantly. |
| BROOKS Molly | | 12 Nov 2013 | L1 Lack of or incorrect equipment/uniform/planner/PE kit | |
| BROOKS Molly | | 15 Nov 2013 | L4 Persistent refusal of an adults request | Whenever I see Molly she is out of a lesson or tutor time. This morning she was out of tutor and I asked her where she was supposed to be / where she was going and why. She refused to asnwer any of my questions and simply walked off. This is a repeat pattern of everytime I encouter Molly across the school. I am concerned that as a prefect, Molly is providing this type of negative attitude and should be a positive, engaged role model for others. |
| BROOKS Molly | | 19 Nov 2013 | L1 Using phone/ipod/headphones without permission | using her mobile phone in ERIC and not reading 18.11.13 |
| BROOKS Molly | | 25 Nov 2013 | L1 No homework | |
| BROOKS Molly | | 11 Dec 2013 | L1 Using phone/ipod/headphones without permission | texting in self study session. |
| BROOKS Molly | | 17 Dec 2013 | L4 Lesson truancy | Molly left the tutor without permission, said she was seeing Miss Cubbage although she was told she could not leave totur. She was also missing from ERIC 16.12.13 and arrived 20 minutes late without a suitable explanation. |
| BROOKS Molly | | 20 Jan 2014 | L3 Failure to produce minimum controlled assessment/coursework in lesson. | Molly was asked to complete an being of topic test for ASd in her absence. Molly decided she could not do any of it and so within 5 minutes gave up and from then she was disruptive, continued to talk when supposed to be silent, she got up and moved around the room. I repeatly tried to help her despite it being a test but without any luck as she did not want to be helped... After being spoken to by V Meyer she did minimal work for about 10 minutes. |
| BROOKS Molly | | 30 Jan 2014 | L1 Lateness to lesson/tutor time | |

| | | | | |
|---|---|---|---|---|
| BROOKS Molly | | 31 Jan 2014 | L4 Persistent refusal of an adults request | Molly refused to complete any work at all in the lesson. She refused to remove her hoodie also despite being asked a number of times |
| BROOKS Molly | | 20 Jan 2014 | L6 Persistent Level 5 breaches | Molly was putting offensive comments on facebook about another student. this has been on going with Molly refusing to remove comments or take responsibilty for her actions. 1 day exclusion. |
| BROOKS Molly | | 07 Feb 2014 | L1 No homework | No homework this week. |
| BROOKS Molly | | 10 Feb 2014 | L4 Lesson truancy | LH on Learning Walk. Molly refused on numerous occasions to return to class, CC also involved after 15 mins both staff refused to continue to chase Molly. |
| BROOKS Molly | | 24 Feb 2014 | L4 Lesson truancy | molly was truanting from assembly after attending tutor. dt set |
| BROOKS Molly | | 24 Feb 2014 | L4 Lesson truancy | Molly truanted lesson 1, in Science?? |
| BROOKS Molly | | 25 Feb 2014 | L4 Lesson truancy | Molly was late to lesson. When she wouldn't sit in seating plan she left the room. |
| BROOKS Molly | | 05 Mar 2014 | L2 Disruption of learning | Molly came into my year 8 class and called one of the class members gay. |
| BROOKS Molly | | 05 Mar 2014 | L2 Disruption of learning | Molly continues to disrupt other students around her despite constant warnings. Moved her to work alone in another room. |
| BROOKS Molly | | 12 Mar 2014 | L3 Refusing an Adult | Molly was in the corridor at breaktime despite not being allowed to be. I asked her repeatedly to leave and she eventually did (after talking back and walking past me and so on). She returned twice more within the same breaktime, each time initially refusing to leave. She was warned her behaviour would lead to a level 3. It was only when she was told she already had a level 3 and was being warned of a level 4 that she left finally. More than one staff member had asked Molly to leave. |
| BROOKS Molly | | 27 Mar 2014 | L2 Other Level 2 incidents | |
| BROOKS Molly | | 28 Mar 2014 | L2 Other Level 2 incidents | Molly was throwing litter down the stair case and some of it was hitting other students. |
| BROOKS Molly | | 02 Apr 2014 | L3 Inappropriate physical contact (not a fight) | throwing water at Shania steer in the coridor at the end of break at the start of P3 |
| BROOKS Molly | | 04 Apr 2014 | L2 Other Level 2 incidents | Molly was involvedv in an incident where a newletter had been ripped up and thr0wn around the corridor, she initially thought this was really funny and tried to walk away but did evenutally pick up the newsletter and placed it in a bin |
| BROOKS Molly | | 04 Apr 2014 | L1 Lateness to lesson/tutor time | late without an excuse. |
| BROOKS Molly | | 24 Apr 2014 | L3 Refusing an Adult | Initally refusing request from C Cubbage at lunchtime, followed instructions after several requests |
| BROOKS Molly | | 25 Apr 2014 | L4 Refusing to hand over phone or electrical device | |
| BROOKS Molly | | 07 May 2014 | L3 Other Level 3 incidents | Wearing her school trousers rolled up and refusing to roll them down |

FAMILY

This is my best friend that sadly passed away this year while I was writing this book. He is my forever best friend and I wish I could cuddle with him one last time! I hope you're proud of me Dex, I love & miss you FOREVER XXXX

Printed in the UK by Cloc Book Print
Clocbookprint.com